Bicycling Magazine's

Training
for Fitness
and Endurance

By the Editors of *Bicycling* Magazine

Rodale Press, Emmaus, Pennsylvania

Printed in the United States of America on acid-free ∞, recycled ♻ paper

Compiled and edited by *Joe Kita*

Production editor: *Jane Sherman*
Copy editor: *Durrae Johanek*
Cover and interior design: *Lisa Farkas*
Cover photo: *John P. Hamel*

If you have any questions or comments concerning this book, please write:
    Rodale Press
    Book Readers' Service
    33 East Minor Street
    Emmaus, PA 18098

Library of Congress Cataloging-in-Publication Data

Bicycling magazine's training for fitness and endurance / by the editors
    of Bicycling magazine.
        p.   cm.
    ISBN 0-87857-899-4   paperback
    1. Cycling–Training.   2. Bicycle racing–Training.   I. Bicycling.
    II. Training for fitness and endurance.
    GV1048.B53   1990
    796.6–dc20   89-77188
                                           CIP

Distributed in the book trade by St. Martin's Press

    8 10 9   paperback

CONTENTS

◼️ INTRODUCTION

What are you capable of as a cyclist? How far can you ride? What speed can you maintain?

I remember when completing 10 miles made me proud. Now, it's barely a warm-up. I recall when a century seemed an unconquerable distance. Now I'm getting curious about *double* centuries. And I remember when veteran pro Jonathan Boyer stunned the Race Across America field in 1985 by crossing the country in nine days, 2 hours, and 6 minutes. The current record? Seventeen hours less, with a seven-day crossing considered reachable.

To speak of limits in cycling is self-defeating. The sport is so accommodating that anyone, given time and proper training, will excel. Indeed, the only constraints placed upon us are those that *we* impose.

This book will help shatter limits. It will help you ride farther and faster and will make you a better cyclist than you ever thought possible. While it's meant to be used immediately, the book also has been designed with the future in mind—follow the training programs and philosophies herein, and a few years from now you'll be looking back on that 10-mile ride or that century or maybe even the Race Across America with a veteran's pride.

Joe Kita, Managing Editor
Bicycling Magazine

Part One
CONDITIONING

◼️1◼️ BE YOUR OWN COACH

Behind most great riders is a great coach. But who's *your* coach? Who studies your talent and shortcomings, prescribes your yearly training, inspires, sympathizes, and gives you the occasional verbal kick in the chamois? If you're like the majority of fitness riders, no one. You coach yourself—and, in most cases, your coach is doing a lousy job.

It's hard to be your own coach. For starters, you're too close to your subject. Good coaches are objective about their athletes and rational about each day's workout. Conversely, the athlete often lets emotion overwhelm reason. Reason says, "Do some hard climbing." But emotion says, "Forget it!" Or, as is often the case with riders bent on improvement, reason demands a rest day but the athlete, physically tired but emotionally wired, does 30 tough miles instead.

Coaching yourself is also difficult if you don't have confidence in your qualifications. Great coaches are charismatic—they believe in their training approach and they sell their riders on it. All the cyclist has to do is follow the program—no second-guessing, no arguing, no choices. But when *you* decide what the day's workout will be, you're apt to have less confidence in it than if those same orders came from a professional coach.

Even experienced racers know the feeling. Cindy Olavarri, for example, was a silver medalist in the 1983 World Championships. "When I was formulating my own program, I was never totally positive that I was doing the right thing," Olavarri says today. The sad truth of the matter is that this lack of confidence is usually justified—most of us don't have the knowledge to be good coaches. And if you're using ineffective training ideas, you may coach yourself right out of cycling.

Some riders, however, know too much. In the past few years, cycling books and magazines have become more common than glass on the road. If the latest article doesn't puncture a cherished training belief, it hypes some super new training plan. A lot of self-coached riders try a program for a month but switch to something completely different when the next article appears. And eventually, buried in a heap of contradictory information, their efforts at self-coaching fail.

"The secret of being successful," 7-Eleven team pro Davis Phinney says, "is the ability to assimilate a lot of information and put it to use in the best possible manner."

It takes time to become a good coach, just as it takes practice to develop bike-handling skills. And when you're on your own, it takes twice as long—you're developing both skills at once. Masters rider Ross Potoff speaks for many when he says, "Having a coach would have saved me a lot of time. I've had to rely on my own instincts. And they weren't always good ones."

Seven Steps to Successful Self-Coaching

1. Set goals. What do you want from cycling? The ability to ride a century in less than 8 hours, or the fortitude to complete a cross-country tour? However lofty or modest your aims, you need to identify them and write them down. When your personal goals are firmly set, every training day has a purpose. You know exactly why you are doing intervals or a long ride or an easy spin. Without clear goals, training seems aimless and it's certainly less effective.

Goals must be realistic. If you have a full-time job or a heavy load of classes, you shouldn't plan on riding 500 miles a week. There isn't enough time or energy to do both successfully, and the quickest way to end up frustrated with your cycling progress is to set goals unrealistically high.

2. Evaluate your talent. Do this objectively and honestly. If you have been riding regularly for a year and still can't stay with the pack on your Sunday ride, the best program in the world probably won't make you a star. You can't get Greg LeMond results out of a Clyde Pudbelly body.

Americans like to believe in the value of hard work, especially in sports. But athletic talent is distributed unequally, and unless your goals correspond to your abilities, you're going to be disappointed. We're not suggesting, however, that you pin your cycling career entirely on the results of a VO_2 max test. The world would be a dreary place without dreams, but make sure yours are rooted in reality.

3. Evaluate your strengths and weaknesses. A good training plan maximizes your cycling talents and fixes shortcomings. Learn your strengths and weaknesses by watching what happens while riding with others, and then do something about it. Are you first in sprints to the city limit sign but last on long rides? Build endurance by adding one or two long, steady rides to your weekly schedule. Do you set the pace forever on the flat but always lose the lead on hills? You need more power. Diet to lower your percentage of body fat and start doing hill repeats, weight training, and big-gear work on an indoor resistance trainer.

4. Ask questions. Get information from experienced cyclists. "Don't be intimidated by anyone," says Phinney. "Be as inquisitive as possible. People like to give advice."

The most helpful riders have usually studied the sport for several years and ride intelligently to maximize less-than-outstanding physical talent. Get a variety of views even if you think your program is going well. As U.S. pro Ron Kiefel notes, "It's good to have second opinions," and one place to find them is at your local bike club—a great place to meet experienced riders.

5. Record your workouts. What works, works; keep a training diary so you can duplicate programs that produce hot streaks. Conversely, when you ride poorly, you'll know what training patterns to avoid.

Each morning, record your pulse so you can spot the upward trend that signals overtraining. Also, weigh yourself to help guard against the chronic dehydration and rapid weight loss that leads to fatigue.

Detail the length of your rides: miles and minutes, the terrain, weather, gears used, and effort. Write how you felt, whether it was "Great!" or just "Rotten." Evaluate this information regularly to see what works and what doesn't—don't make the common mistake of keeping a diary just to build an impressive mileage total. Within your written words is information as valuable as anything a coach can provide.

6. Chart your improvement. Getting better is the name of the game. To be sure your program is working, you need a reasonably accurate method of gauging improvement.

Sheer mileage is a useful but unsophisticated indicator. Early in your career, you can review your diary to see if you can handle more miles. If you rode 2,000 miles last year and increased to 2,500 this season without undue fatigue, you can confidently push toward 3,000 next year. LeMond increased his mileage 10 to 15 percent annually during his developmental years, a reasonable rate for any cyclist. The same percentage works well for weekly mileage increases in the early season. For example, if you ride 80 miles the first week in April, you'd risk injury and fatigue by jumping to 120 the next, but you could almost certainly handle 90.

Endurance mileage isn't the whole story, of course. You want to get faster, too, so you need a way to measure your improvements in speed. Time trialing is the simplest and most accurate method. Find a 5- to 10-mile course near your home, ride it all-out once a month, and compare times to see if your workouts are working. Take wind and weather into account, and remember to go easy the day before each attempt so you're rested. Fatigue should not be a factor.

7. Add spice to your training. Many of us become obsessive about training and spend every spare minute riding, thinking about riding, or working on the bike. This gets old quickly. To avoid it, take a tip from world-class coaches and divide the year into distinct training periods or cycles. Vary your weekly schedule, too, so you aren't doing the same thing on the same day every week. Occasionally, do something offbeat—dash down wooded trails on a mountain bike, for example, or go touring if racing is normally your preference. And if you're feeling the old zip has been zapped by too much riding, take a week off. Several days away from the bike can do wonders to revitalize your attitude and performance.

2 GETTING READY TO RIDE

It's spring! The sky is blue, the birds are singing, and your bike is out of the cellar. You hop on, pedal away—and soon discover that your legs burn, your lungs ache, and your bottom hurts. Winter, with its inclement weather and short days, can put the whammy on an ambitious fitness schedule, so you're not alone in your early-season struggles. The goal, then? To make maximum progress in minimum time, without sore muscles or excessive fatigue.

Heart and Lungs

We'll start at the heart of the matter—your cardiovascular system.

For fast recreational/endurance riding, the priority is building a mileage base. This is true even if you worked the winter away on an indoor trainer. There's no substitute for pedaling against gravity and wind.

Start slowly, especially if you didn't do much riding in winter. Even top racers who ride almost year-round like to have four to six weeks of aerobically paced riding in their legs before beginning hard training—a worthy goal for every cyclist.

Accumulate these early miles in a low gear, at a cadence of 90 to 110 pedal revolutions per minute (rpm). Develop a smooth, supple stroke. Reasonably flat terrain is best, but if your local roads are Himalayan, use a granny gear and spin up the climbs. As your base miles accumulate, use larger gears, lengthen the rides, and include more hills. Aim for the level of conditioning necessary for the type of rides you want to do this season.

Consider using a heart rate monitor. If you pedal at 70 to 85 percent of your maximum heart rate, you'll build aerobic power without risking injury or the chronic fatigue that comes from trying to go too hard too soon. Greg LeMond wears a monitor on all training rides to, in his words, "make sure I'm going hard enough to get some benefit. It's easy to slow down and let your heart rate drop below 65 or 70 percent."

You can also check your heart rate manually. Find your pulse on the carotid artery to the right of the Adam's apple, count the beats for 15 seconds and multiply by four. To estimate your maximum heart rate, subtract your age from 220 (for men) or 226 (for women).

Legs

While you're tuning your heart and lungs, you're also conditioning your legs. Steady spinning accomplishes this, helped along by the hill work you add gradually. But for variety, try some off-road riding. And if you've been on a winter weight training program, continue with squats and other leg exercises, especially if bad weather restricts riding.

Once you have a low-gear base of about one-third your estimated total yearly mileage, it's time to work on power. The best way to build powerful pistons is interval training. But be careful—this is also the quickest way to develop a hearty dislike for cycling.

Avoid structured interval workouts—each sprint lasting a minute, each rest period 30 seconds, for example. Instead think of "recreational intervals," a good name for random efforts lasting between 30 seconds and 3 minutes. Do these whenever you feel like it. Sprint away from a stop sign, jam over a short hill, time trial the last mile into town. During group rides you do an interval every time you take a pull.

Unless you're a dedicated racer bent on improvement, endless repeats of timed, gut-busting efforts will make you wish winter would return.

Emphasize time trials in your training. These extended high-speed efforts tune your legs differently than intervals because they require a constant, steady pace for the distance.

Establish several courses between 5 and 10 miles and time yourself on one every week. Or participate in time trials held by a local bike club. The extended effort will elevate your fitness and help you develop a smooth, efficient riding style. And since it's just you against the clock—time trials are called "the race of truth"—they are also a great way to gauge your progress.

Arms and Shoulders

Your arms and shoulders aren't just along for the ride. They stabilize your upper body and become increasingly important the harder you pedal and the farther you ride. Strong arms help you pull on the handlebar to counterbalance the power of your legs. Remember, you pedal with your legs but ride with your entire body.

Some cyclists increase upper-body strength with winter weight training but stop lifting when spring arrives. By midsummer their extra strength is gone. But just one set of upper-body exercises two or three times a week is all it takes to hang on to those winter gains. The following program can be done in about 15 minutes with a standard barbell set, a bench or table for back extensions, and a pull-up bar. Consult a weight training coach or authoritative manual for in-depth descriptions of specific techniques and safe execution.

Use the ride for your warm-up. Immediately afterward, loosen your upper body with stretching or light calisthenics. Load the barbell with a weight that permits 15 to 25 repetitions of each exercise before you begin to lose form. The objective is to build muscular endurance, something best accomplished with high reps with light weights. Do the exercises in this order:

1. Military press
2. Upright row
3. Neck bridges
4. Bent-over row
5. Sit-ups
6. Shoulder shrugs
7. Pull-ups
8. Back extensions

During midseason, you can conserve your finite energy stores by reducing upper-body work even further. Cut back to pull-ups, sit-ups, and abdominal exercises only.

Lower Back and Stomach

Your body hinges at the lower back. Because of the riding posture, many cyclists suffer from sore lower back muscles on long rides. Back extensions will strengthen this area, as will barbell exercises like good mornings and stiff-leg dead lifts. Weak stomach muscles are often a primary contributor to back pain, so sit-ups and crunches should be regular parts of your workout, too.

Neck

Don't neglect your neck—it supports your most important piece of equipment. If you crash, a strong neck may prevent serious injury. Strengthen it with simple exercises such as the wrestling bridge—lie on your back and then arch to place the weight on neck and legs. Other options include using a weighted neck harness (available at sporting goods stores) or a four-way neck machine (at health clubs). Stronger neck muscles have an everyday benefit, too. They carry the weight of your head and helmet during long rides more easily, virtually eliminating neck and upper-shoulder fatigue.

Muscles and Ligaments

Top riders differ on the need for stretching. Some do it regularly, others mean to get in the habit but don't budget the time. Nonetheless it's probably wise to stretch lightly before and after each ride, especially to loosen your lower back and hamstrings. These areas can become tight and sore from cycling. Always remember: Stretch slowly, without bouncing, and don't force a stretch to the point of pain.

Fat Stores

If you're carrying a few extra pounds, the winter weight will probably come off naturally as you ride more. But if you decide nature needs some help, don't cut calories drastically. You won't enjoy riding if you aren't eating enough to replenish muscle fuel (glycogen) each day. To drop fat, the best way is to cut fat out of your diet. Emphasize carbohydrates—your primary source of glycogen—and eliminate salad dressing, butter, and fatty baked goods. The pounds will roll off as the miles roll by.

Rear End

A sore bottom puts an end to as many rides as tired legs and empty lungs. But gradually increasing mileage will help you callous in the right places. If you still have problems, check your riding position. A saddle that's too high, for example, will make you rock when you pedal, which irritates tender tissue, while a saddle with its nose slanted down will make you slide forward. If all else fails, you may need to try a different saddle. One that's slightly narrower or wider may fit your unique anatomy better than the bun-crusher you're using. Gel- or foam-filled saddles also may relieve painful pressure but can cost significantly more than standard seats.

Use quality, chamois-lined cycling shorts that don't have seams in potentially irritating places. Keep the chamois scrupulously clean by washing the shorts after every ride. And use a chamois cream to reduce friction and irritation. Coat the chamois and your crotch before each ride.

Fitting It All Together

How can you fit all this training into an already busy life? Here's a sample schedule to use after you've finished several weeks of steady, low-gear spinning. It includes enough cycling to get you ready for summer yet provides plenty of time for other responsibilities and rest.

Monday: No ride. Recover from weekend cycling.

Tuesday: Ride between 45 minutes and 2 hours at a varied pace, depending on your fitness and available time. Weight train after the ride.

Wednesday: No ride. Do a light alternate exercise such as walking.

Thursday: Ride between 45 minutes and 2 hours. Include intervals, hills, time trials. Occasionally ride with a group, if possible.

Friday: No ride. Do bike maintenance.

Saturday: Ride at a comfortable pace for an hour or two. Weight train afterward.

Sunday: Ride with a group or do a long solo ride at a varied pace. Work toward the conditioning necessary for centuries, races, long tours—whatever your season holds.

3 OLYMPIC STRETCHING FOR YOUR BODY AND MIND

By Mark Gorski
1984 Olympic Gold Medalist

If you want to improve as a cyclist you need to do more than just ride your bike. You have to stretch body and mind in ways that supplement and enhance your normal training.

Stretching your body means doing a set of muscle-loosening exercises before and after every workout. Ironically, stretching was never high on my list of priorities until I saw the East German sprinters in 1979—my first year of international competition. I was amazed at how these heavily muscled giants became human pretzels in warm-ups, and I realized how devastating such a combination of strength and elasticity could be. In fact, my own sprinting ability and resistance to injury improved dramatically after I began a regular stretching program.

Stretching the mind is a similar concept. Mental preparedness has helped me ride better on many occasions, but most notably during the finals of the match sprint at the 1984 Olympics. At a press conference following the semifinals, a reporter asked Nelson Vails, who would race me the next day, if he would be satisfied with the silver medal. Nelson said yes, admitting he was pleased to have reached this point. But I said I had been waiting for this moment for years and didn't come for the silver medal—I wanted the gold or nothing at all.

This was a bold statement, but I had often imagined winning the gold medal. I had pictured every detail. I had seen every face in the crowd. I had rehearsed the strategy of each ride. And I had envisioned the incredible excitement and joy of Olympic victory.

I was doing it naturally but this type of dreaming is what's known among sports psychologists as mental rehearsal or visualization. You've probably done it yourself many times. It can be a powerful confidence-builder, but it can also generate stress. Too often, riders visualize an upcoming tour, century, or race and see themselves experiencing a difficult time or even failing. This generates more pressure and, many times, reduces performance.

I don't believe Nelson ever rehearsed winning the Olympic gold. He may have dreamed of competing but never winning. As a result, the pressure of the moment overwhelmed him. But for me, it was merely a fulfillment of what was supposed to happen. I was physically *and* mentally prepared.

Visualization can work for you just as well. Find a quiet place during the day or go to bed a little earlier each night. Then, relax and begin imagining yourself taking part in the event. Try to see every detail, including each turn along the route, the gear you're riding in, even the faces of your competitors (if there are any). These images should be real—feel the wind, and the sting of sweat in your eyes. When I visualize an important sprint, I actually get stomach butterflies and sweaty palms.

Most important, picture yourself doing well—even to the point of feeling joy when you win. Live the ride two or three times each day and again immediately before it happens.

Positive mental rehearsal minimizes stress and builds confidence by supplying the subconscious assurance that you've done it all before.

A Gold Medal Stretch

Once you're mentally ready, you have to prepare your muscles to do the job they've been assigned. This is where stretching your body comes into play, and it is important for several reasons. First and foremost, it helps prevent injury. Pulled muscles are rare in cycling but they do happen. I pulled a hamstring muscle one cool, damp day in Belgium, an injury that kept me from being 100 percent for several weeks. It could have been prevented if I had been stretching regularly.

Second, stretching reduces your warm-up time. How many of you have gone for an early morning ride without having stretched and, on that first hill, felt as if your legs were blown up like balloons? Stretching "prestresses" the muscles, enhancing blood flow, oxygenation, and suppleness, all of which help you warm up quicker.

Third, stretching improves performance by creating an efficient muscle system. If your legs are tight, for instance, other muscles are recruited to help do the work. This crossover wastes energy.

Keep the following things in mind before starting your stretching program. A successful program is a consistent one—you will realize much more improvement by stretching 15 minutes every day than 30 minutes every third day. Stretch before training rides, races, and even lifting weights. Make it a regular part of your workout routine.

Likewise, get into the habit of stretching after a workout. I immediately get off my bike and spend about 10 minutes stretching. This helps my body cool down properly and keeps my muscles from tightening up or cramping. It also helps keep them loose for the next day's workout.

Always stretch with smooth, gentle movements. Do not stretch until it hurts, and do not bounce. To derive the most benefit, do the suggested exercises every day, even when you don't ride. Except for the upper-body stretches, hold each one for 20 to 30 seconds so the muscles have the opportunity to relax in each position. This may be difficult to do initially, but it's important. And remember to duplicate the exercise for the muscles on the other side of your body. Do the stretches in the order described.

1. Trunk twisters. With your arms extended, gently twist your torso left and right. This loosens your upper and lower back muscles. Extend as far as possible on each rotation. When you reach the limit on both sides, hold this part of the stretch for 20 to 30 seconds.

2. Side bends. With your feet shoulder-width apart, place one hand on your hip and extend the other arm as far down your leg as possible. Hold this position. It stretches your lower back and the oblique muscles on the sides of your abdomen.

3. Windmills. Raise your arms to the side at shoulder height and begin making large, slow circles with both your arms—first in one direction, then the other. Inhale and exhale deeply while doing this.

4. Reverse hurdles stretch. Basically, this is the same as a conventional hurdles stretch except that one leg is tucked in rather than out, thus minimizing pressure on the knee. Hold this for 20 to 30 seconds to really stretch the hamstring.

Photograph 1-1. Reverse hurdles stretch.

5. Knee-to-chest. While on your back, bring your knee close to your chest and hold it there. This stretches the hamstrings and gluteal muscles.

Photograph 1-2. Knee-to-chest.

6. Human pretzel. Once you figure out how to arrange your body, you'll be able to stretch the iliotibial band that runs along the side of each thigh. This tends to shorten with cycling (and running).

7. Sprinter's stretch. This may seem like a variation of the knee-to-chest, but you'll find it stretches the muscles of the straightened leg as much if not more than the muscles in the bent leg.

Two other exercises are the calf stretch and the quadriceps stretch. To do the former, stand facing a wall with your feet staggered but flat on the ground. Extend your arms for support and lean forward. Keep your back leg straight, and you'll feel the calf muscles stretch. Hold for 20 to 30 seconds, then repeat for the other leg.

To stretch your quadriceps, stand on one leg, bend the other knee back, and grasp your foot. Then, slowly pull it toward your rear end. You'll feel the muscles in the front of the leg—the real cycling pistons—begin to stretch. You'll need to hold onto something for balance when performing this stretch.

Photograph 1-3.
Human pretzel.

Photograph 1-4. Sprinter's stretch.

4 TRAINING FOR A CENTURY

Dean Stewart, 33, of Fort Polk, Louisiana, wasn't elated when he finished his first century ride. He was too exhausted. In fact, he almost abandoned the ride during the final 25 miles. But instead of souring him on distance riding, the experience drove him to try again in two more centuries—completing one in 6 hours and 15 minutes. This season his goal is to break 6 hours and maybe even try a double century (200 miles).

"I like discovering abilities I didn't think I had," says Stewart. "I've become a much more confident rider."

Like many cyclists, Stewart admits to being undertrained for his first century. And like so many others, the humbling experience that resulted encouraged him to prepare more fully for the next one.

But what kind of training and mileage base is needed if you're to actually enjoy a century? Karen Roy, a former nationally ranked sprinter who is now an exercise physiologist, coaches elite and beginning cyclists. She says, "You can achieve a fitness base by riding 100 miles per week. From there, you can increase mileage during a six- to eight-week period to the point where you can comfortably ride a century."

According to Roy, a first-time century rider at the start of a ten-week training program would need 7- to 10-mile workouts four evenings a week, a 40-mile ride on Saturday, and a 25-miler on Sunday. Two weeks before the century, she recommends attempting at least a 75-mile ride on the weekend to gauge if the preparation has been adequate.

Roy further recommends setting time or average-speed goals during the longer weekend rides in order to develop pacing skills. But she cautions against adding more than 10 extra miles at a time to any long ride.

Ample training mileage can result in a surprisingly enjoyable first century. "It was a feeling of euphoria and accomplishment," recalls Craig Jeffs, 37, of Brigham City, Utah. "I was tired, but not hurting, as I thought I'd be."

Despite bad weather, Jeffs completed his first century in

slightly less than 8 hours. Following *Bicycling* magazine's Century Challenge training program (see table 1-1, schedule 1), he was logging 150 miles per week just prior to the event. "I felt good about the training and went into the century knowing I could do it," he says.

As a teacher and father of five, Jeffs also had to shoehorn his cycling in between job and family. To do that he used what he calls "one-way cycling." Instead of riding time-consuming loop or out-and-back routes on the weekends, he arranged to meet his family at a relative's house or a state park. At the end of the day he'd return home by car. "I'd get my training in and spend time with the family, too," he says.

According to Jeffs, one-way cycling also works on weekdays. For instance, early in the season, he'd take his bike to work in a car pool, then ride home in the afternoon.

Customizing your century training program is crucial. But trying to do too much too soon, or in too limited an amount of time, can be just as debilitating as undertraining. Staleness, fatigue, slow recovery, and even injury can result. The best way to prevent overtraining, says Roy, is to keep a training log. She suggests rating how you feel before and after each ride, using a simple A, B, C, D, or F system. "If Cs and Ds are showing up often, you should back off," she says. "You're not recovering well enough to benefit from your training."

Other signs of overtraining include a resting pulse—taken right after you get out of bed in the morning—that's 10 percent above normal, and restless sleep. To help combat overtraining, Roy recommends varying training partners and routes. "Be on the lookout for new places to ride," she says. "And be willing to put the bike in the car and go somewhere after work if necessary to get to good training roads."

Experts say recovery is an integral part of proper preparation. In fact, what you do after your training rides can actually enhance the benefits of the workout. Ken Fuller, a former national-level racer who's a cycling coach in Anaheim, California, says stretching before and after rides is crucial. He also recommends self-massage. It promotes muscle recovery and restful sleep while discouraging cramps.

To massage yourself, lie on the floor and extend and elevate a leg against a wall. Work it for 5 minutes, starting at the foot and progressing to the thigh, always stroking toward the heart. Repeat for the other leg.

"You'll learn to feel which muscles are tight and how to knead them," says Fuller. "It'll feel good and speed recovery."

Using the Schedules

To help riders prepare for *Bicycling* magazine's annual Century Challenge, we devised two training programs, shown in table 1-1. We're pleased to say we heard from many readers who followed these schedules and had excellent results. Each offers an optimal mileage buildup yet fits into a busy life.

TABLE 1-1.
Schedule 1

Goal: To Ride 100 Miles

Week	Mon.	Tues.	Wed.	Thurs.	Fri.	Sat.	Sun.	Total Weekly Mileage
	Easy	Pace	Brisk		Pace	Pace	Pace	
1	6	10	12	Off	10	30	9	77
2	7	11	13	Off	11	34	10	86
3	8	13	15	Off	13	38	11	98
4	8	14	17	Off	14	42	13	108
5	9	15	19	Off	15	47	14	119
6	11	15	21	Off	15	53	16	131
7	12	15	24	Off	15	59	18	143
8	13	15	25	Off	15	65	20	153
9	15	15	25	Off	15	65	20	155
10	15	15	25	Off	10	5 Easy	100	170

If you're new to distance riding, follow schedule 1. It's designed to help riders complete their first century. It assumes you've been riding an average of 45 to 50 miles per week. If you've been riding more than that—75 miles a week, for example—try schedule 2. It should help you achieve a personal best in your next century.

In each schedule, "easy" means a leisurely ride, mainly to recover from a previous day's hard workout. "Pace" means simulating the speed you want to maintain for the century. And "brisk" means a quick tempo that's faster than century pace. If your century is on a Saturday, move back the final week's training one day (for example, take Wednesday off, ride 10 miles Thursday, ride 5 miles Friday).

Schedule 2
Goal: A Century with Strength to Spare

Week	Mon.	Tues.	Wed.	Thurs.	Fri.	Sat.	Sun.	Total Weekly Mileage
	Easy	Pace	Brisk		Pace	Pace	Pace	
1	10	12	14	Off	12	40	15	103
2	10	13	15	Off	13	44	17	112
3	10	15	17	Off	15	48	18	123
4	11	16	19	Off	16	53	20	135
5	12	18	20	Off	18	59	22	149
6	13	19	23	Off	19	64	24	162
7	14	20	25	Off	20	71	27	177
8	16	20	27	Off	20	75	29	187
9	17	20	30	Off	20	75	32	194
10	19	20	30	Off	10	5 Easy	100	184

TABLE 1-2.
Century Time Goals

Avg. mph	Time (hr:min)	Avg. mph	Time (hr:min)
10.0	10:00	18.0	5:33
10.5	9:31	18.5	5:24
11.0	9:05	19.0	5:16
11.5	8:42	19.5	5:08
12.0	8:20	20.0	5:00
12.5	8:00	20.5	4:53
13.0	7:42	21.0	4:46
13.5	7:24	21.5	4:39
14.0	7:09	22.0	4:33
14.5	6:54	22.5	4:27
15.0	6:40	23.0	4:21
15.5	6:27	23.5	4:15
16.0	6:15	24.0	4:10
16.5	6:04	24.5	4:05
17.0	5:53	25.0	4:00
17.5	5:43		

5 TRAINING
FOR A DOUBLE CENTURY

By Chris Kostman
Race Across America Veteran

One of the great rewards of cycling is being able to ride farther and faster each season. When you reach the point where you can ride a brisk century or comfortably cover more than 100 miles, you might consider doing a double century—200 miles in one day.

A double century isn't just two consecutive centuries. It's a unique event that requires a different strategy and more careful preparation. Fatigue is a major factor, and proper nutrition is crucial. Conditions vary more—you may start in sunshine and finish 12 hours later in darkness and rain. You'll find parts of the ride painful and battle desires to quit. You'll probably consume 20 bottles of liquid and 6,000 calories or more. But you'll also have the satisfaction of extending the limits of your mind and body, and joining a select group of cyclists who have "done a double."

My first double century—completed when I was 16—typifies the problems that can arise. I'd ridden eight centuries before this, with a best time of 5 hours, 45 minutes. I reasoned I could double the distance without any problem.

In preparation I logged as many miles as possible, often riding at dawn to get in 50 miles before school. I did a few centuries and several races. During the final week I tried to eat well and get plenty of sleep.

I arrived at the start at 5:00 A.M., only to see all the participants departing into the darkness. I hurried to the registration table, but was told that because I had no lights I couldn't start until sunrise. Someone offered me a small, battery-powered light and I was off, pushing a big gear in order to catch the pack.

Eventually I settled into a moderate pace and joined a group of riders for company and a break from the wind. It was a good move—with their help I covered the first 100 miles quickly, arriving at the turnaround in about 7 hours. There, I stopped for my first real break, which lasted nearly 30 minutes.

But once I was back on the road, I discovered my muscles were painfully tight. I joined another paceline to help pass the miles. After several hours I could no longer stay with them. As the sun set it began to get cold, and my light wasn't bright enough to even read the map. I cycled alone in the darkness. My knees began to hurt from having pushed too hard earlier in the day. I was underlit, underdressed, and underfed. I crossed the finish line in 14½ hours—a moment I'll never forget.

Since that day I've done numerous double centuries, as

well as triple and quadruple centuries. My passion for distance led me to do the 200-mile Iditabike mountain bike race in Alaska and two Race Across America qualifiers (700 and 550 miles, respectively). In 1987 I completed RAAM (3,129 miles) in ten days, 23 hours, and 58 minutes. At age 20, I was the youngest rider to ever finish the race.

To this day I still use double centuries to gauge my fitness level. Since that difficult and rewarding first double, I've lowered my time to 9:17. It took years of training, racing, and experimentation to enable me to cover 200 miles so quickly and efficiently. Here are some of the things I learned.

Planning and Doing

A double century requires long hours in the saddle, so it's important to be comfortable on your bike and have an efficient pedaling style. Consult with a bike shop that uses the Fit Kit or a similar bicycle sizing system to ensure that your riding position is correct and your cleats are properly adjusted. If changes are required, give yourself time to adapt.

As you train, concentrate on form. Maintain a brisk cadence (90 to 100 pedal revolutions per minute). If possible, have an experienced rider critique your pedaling style, or videotape yourself. You should pedal in smooth circles, and your knees should move vertically in one plane. Riding rollers is an excellent way to improve form.

Ride at least five days each week, gradually increasing intensity and mileage. Keep a training log, noting distance, time, average speed, and terrain. Also record what you eat, how you feel, weight, and resting heart rate. The latter (taken before rising each morning) is an excellent fitness indicator that can alert you to overtraining. When I'm stressed or at my lowest fitness level my heart zooms along at 55 beats per minute. When I'm at peak fitness, it dips to 38 or lower.

Your weekly program should vary in terrain and distance. Few double centuries are flat, so include one or two days of climbing. Do a fast-paced club ride once a week to increase speed and improve group riding skills. Maintain this program for at least six weeks.

A basic weekly schedule might go like this:

Saturday and Sunday: Long, high-intensity rides, 60 to 80 miles per day.

Monday: Easy spin, 15 to 25 miles.

Tuesday: Rest.

Wednesday through Friday: Gradually increase mileage and intensity, 30 to 60 miles per day.

For variety, try off-road riding, racing, or a triathlon. This is important, because if training gets boring it will also get less intense and less frequent. Cross-training also enhances overall fitness, which is vital to fighting fatigue in long events. My weekly schedule often includes running, hiking, weight lifting, tae kwon do, racquetball, and Ultimate Frisbee. I'm convinced these activities help my riding. Stretching also helps fight fatigue and prevents cramping. But an athlete's body also needs rest, so do nothing strenuous at least one day each week.

Throughout your preparation, keep your goal in mind and visualize yourself achieving it. Cycling performance is 50 percent mental. It's determination that will see you through your training and enable you to cross the finish line.

As the day of the double approaches, gauge your fitness. Try to comfortably complete a ride of 200 kilometers (124 miles) or ride back-to-back centuries one weekend. Ideally, you should do this with two weeks to go. Your time in this test will give you a rough idea of how to pace yourself in the double century.

You're not likely to improve much in the last few days, so don't overdo it in training. Also, now is the time to make sure your bike is working properly. It would be unfortunate not to finish because of a mechanical problem, so have questionable parts replaced.

Nutrition is vital during the last week. Load up on carbohydrates and fluids. I drink a gallon of water on each of these crucial days. Try to get enough sleep as well.

On the day of the double, allow plenty of time to travel to the start and register (if possible, preregister). Stay in a hotel the night before if the event is far from home. Eat a small, simple breakfast, but avoid all food 20 to 30 minutes before the start, as it may upset your stomach.

Leave yourself enough time to stretch and loosen up. I prefer not to ride too much beforehand for fear of colliding with another distracted rider. Instead, use the first few miles of the event as your warm-up. Finally, check your equipment to be sure you're fully prepared.

I recommend carrying a small tool kit, two spare tubes, patch kit, folding tire, two or three large water bottles, emergency food such as a candy bar (in case you "bonk"), cycle-computer or watch, sunblock and medical supplies, identification, money, and a route sheet. If you anticipate riding in darkness, bring a high-quality cycling light. Your clothing should include a helmet, sunglasses, arm and leg warmers, windbreaker, and gloves.

Some events are mass-start, while others allow you to leave when you please. In a mass-start, don't bother trying to get to the front. It's too congested and dangerous. Be careful when the riders roll out—accidents often occur here.

During the first 10 miles, stay off the large chainring. Once you're warm try joining a paceline of smooth, safe riders traveling at a speed that doesn't make you labor. This will help you go faster, as well as provide good company. Don't overlap wheels with other riders and keep away from those who seem unsteady. Eventually you'll find a group that suits you.

As the miles pass, the important things to keep in mind are nutrition, hydration, comfort, and pace. Try to consume 300 calories per hour. (A piece of fruit, for example, has roughly 100 calories. A bran muffin has 150.) Obey the adage that you should drink before you're thirsty and eat before you're hungry.

Many riders consume a combination of fruit, cookies, muffins, and granola bars. However, keeping your energy stores high with these foods requires a lot of eating. You may also find your energy level varies considerably on such a sugary diet. To avoid these problems I use commercially available carbohydrate drinks such as Exceed. They're a well-balanced source of energy that the body can utilize quickly. If you choose a 100 percent liquid diet, it's imperative that you have experience with it prior to the event to avoid possible digestive problems.

Hydration is another vital component in maintaining energy.

I drink one bottle of water per hour in addition to my liquid food. This is a lot of drinking, but it's necessary. Other drinks should not be substituted for plain water.

Try to stay relaxed during the ride. Keep spinning. Get out of the saddle frequently to stretch your back. When you do stand, shift to a higher gear to maintain your speed. Well-padded gloves are helpful in fighting numbness, as is changing hand positions frequently. Shoes with Velcro closures allow you to alter the pressure on your feet while insoles or orthotics help avoid "hot foot." Wear comfortable, well-padded shorts. You might also benefit from a gel-type saddle.

During the ride, use efficient pacing. Ideally, a double should not consist of one 5-hour and one 7-hour century, but two 6-hour centuries. Don't ride in a paceline that is beyond your ability, and pay attention to your current and average speeds. Use your rest time to eat, wash, and stretch, and don't overeat. After finishing, have a good meal, drink plenty of fluids, and stretch to reduce soreness.

Remember, if the double century becomes too easy, there's always the triple, quadruple, Paris-Brest-Paris, RAAM. . . .

■6■ TRAINING FOR A TOUR

For many touring cyclists, the return of warm weather and long days awakens an urge to take to the road in search of excitement, adventure, discovery, and companionship. But be careful: Without adequate preparation, you may find what you seek.

Consider the excitement of realizing your bike handles far differently on a steep descent with 50 pounds in the panniers; the adventure of grinding unsteadily through deepening twilight toward a distant campsite with legs that decided to quit 10 miles ago; the discovery well into a planned coast-to-coast ride that your favorite saddle is really quite hard and narrow, your handlebar gets farther away each day, and your gearing is suitable for motor-pacing, not loaded touring; and the companionship of the sympathetic Greyhound bus driver with whom you share the woes of your aborted tour as you motor home days ahead of schedule.

No sensible person would consider entering the Boston Marathon or stepping into the English Channel or touching gloves with Mike Tyson without plenty of preparation for the task at hand. Likewise, cyclists embarking on an extended tour (any self-sufficient ride lasting more than two days) should already be reasonably strong and fit. While determination might get you through a weekend tour, a longer trip demands a higher level of fitness if it's going to be enjoyed.

To gauge your current status and determine how much training you might need, Bryant Stamford, Ph.D., director of the University of Louisville's exercise physiology lab, recommends a simple test: Well in advance of your departure date, determine the average daily mileage for your tour and see if you can ride this distance two or three times a week.

If you're like most *Bicycling* magazine readers, you average 50 miles a week. This is a healthy foundation, but it probably won't generate the endurance you need. For optimum touring fitness, you'll have to increase your weekly mileage, as well as the length and intensity of some of your rides.

Dr. Stamford suggests a weekly training schedule that alternates two or three typical touring rides (normal distance and pace) with one or two short, high-intensity workouts. These might include out-of-saddle attacks on hills, flatland sprints, or time trials. One day a week should be reserved for a long ride. This will build even more endurance and accustom you to extended periods in the saddle. Most local clubs hold recreational rides every weekend. These are perfect for augmenting your training, as well as being a lot of fun.

If your schedule can't accommodate extra time on the bike, try commuting to work. Or if the weather doesn't cooperate when you do have the time, duplicate these long/easy, short/hard workouts on an indoor resistance trainer.

If the mileage you should be doing is quite a bit more than you're used to, Dr. Stamford suggests working gradually toward your goal. Start by increasing your total mileage 10 percent a week. If your body responds well, try a 15 percent jump the next week. Conversely, if the additional mileage leaves you feeling exhausted, don't be afraid to take a day off or even reduce your training.

If you're more than 30 years old, Dr. Stamford recommends taking a stress test before beginning any event-specific training program, regardless of whether your doctor thinks it's necessary. "He may not be used to dealing with athletes," Dr. Stamford explains. "Training for an event is more rigorous than just deciding to start exercising. The training schedule drives you, instead of you driving the training. . . . It can get pretty tough."

Listen to Your Heart

To make this conditioning program even more effective, arrange the workouts according to your optimum training heart rate. Begin by estimating your maximum pulse rate, achieved by subtracting your age from 220 if you're male, 226 if you're female. The next step is to determine your resting pulse rate. Upon waking, count your heartbeats for 15 seconds by feeling the pulse at your neck. Multiply by four. Do this on several consecutive mornings and then average the results to determine your resting pulse.

Next, find your training threshold by taking 60 percent of your maximum heart rate reserve (MHRR). To calculate this value, subtract your resting pulse from your estimated maximum rate, multiply by 0.6, and add your resting pulse rate to the result. For example, a 30-year-old male with a resting pulse of 60 has an MHRR of 138 beats per minute ($220 - 30 = 190; 190 - 60 = 130; 130 \times 0.6 = 78; 78 + 60 = 138$).

This is the minimum heart rate this person should maintain during each 30-minute (or longer) training session in order to improve aerobic capacity. Of course, the higher the heart rate, the greater the training effect. If 60 percent of MHRR feels too easy, substitute 70 or 75 percent in the formula. As you get fitter, you'll have to really tackle the hills or blaze along on the flats to reach this level. If 75 percent is still too easy, forget your plans for a leisurely tour—go enter the Race Across America!

When cycling, it's usually easier to take your pulse at the

carotid artery beside the Adam's apple. For absolute accuracy, invest in a pulse monitor. A less precise method—but one that research indicates is usually accurate enough—is perceived exertion: How does the pace feel? Easy, hard, impossible to maintain? Training at 60 percent of your MHRR should seem easy. Conversely, an 85 percent effort should exhaust you within 30 minutes.

Although some exercise physiologists contend that heart rate training is unnecessary for those embarking upon a long-term, high-mileage conditioning program, it is useful for those wishing to derive the most benefit from the least amount of exercise time. In addition, it is a valuable tool for keeping motivated cyclists from exercising too hard.

Use this information in your weekly program by exercising at or above your 60 percent training heart rate. Maintain it for the duration of your long weekend ride and on the days you duplicate your touring pace. Go well above it (75 percent or more) on high-intensity days. Organizing your workouts in this manner will ensure continued improvement in aerobic capacity.

Strength to Endure

Aerobic fitness is important for touring cyclists, but it's only part of the package. You'll also need enough muscle strength to crank that loaded bike up a long mountain road and keep it under control on the winding descent. The best way to become a stronger, more skilled cyclist? In Eddy Merckx's words, "Ride lots."

If your goal is touring fitness, you shouldn't be riding just any bike. Different muscles come into play when riding a loaded bicycle as opposed to a 22-pound racer. It takes more upper-body strength to control a loaded bike when cornering, especially if much of the weight is over the rear wheel. As a result, plan to start riding your touring bike with full panniers weeks before leaving.

While there's no substitute for the task-specific isometric conditioning of pulling on the handlebar, push-ups and sit-ups will help strengthen the upper body and back muscles so important to loaded touring. Riding a mountain bike off-road will also build your shoulders, arms, and hands. And it's a lot more fun than kissing the carpet 50 times a night.

In training, ride with full panniers to familiarize yourself with the idiosyncrasies of handling a loaded bike. Descending is one area that demands particular attention. Because of the extra weight, use only top-notch brakes and apply them harder and sooner when entering corners or stopping. As on any bike, brakes should be used intermittently to prevent glazing the pads and overheating the rims.

While you're mastering handling, also fine-tune riding position and gearing. A handlebar stem that's the perfect height and extension for quick and fast 25-mile training rides might promote discomfort during a long, 75-mile day in the saddle. Gearing, meanwhile, should be the result of much prudence. Determine the lowest gear ratio you will need and then add a couple of teeth to the largest rear cog, or subtract a couple from the granny ring up front. The lowest ratio should be your bail-out gear, to be used only in near-vertical emergencies. Even twiddling along in a 20-inch gear beats pushing a loaded bike uphill.

A 50-pound load won't allow you the luxury of standing and working the bike from side to side, so get used to climbing while seated and spinning your granny gear. A 1-to-1 gear ratio (i.e., 28-tooth chainring and 28-tooth rear cog) is the minimum if your route has hills. Lower gearing—a larger rear cog and/or smaller inner chainring—is wise for mountainous routes.

Training and practice will ensure that your tour doesn't come to an untimely end because of unexpected aches or unwilling legs, but inadequate mental preparation has ended more tours than all physical difficulties combined. We're not just talking about the know-how to fix mechanical problems, although if you can't repair a flat, replace a broken spoke or cable, or true a wheel—you'd better learn. We're talking about cultivating a state of mind that's braced for dreary weather, headwinds, balky cook stoves, unfriendly natives, and fitful nights in damp and musty sleeping bags.

What's more, even the best of friends together under the rigors of a long, hard tour can end up full of resentment at their comrades' personal habits.

Despite the lure of the open road, extended touring isn't

for every cyclist. If you love to ride hard and fast in anticipation of a gourmet meal and a soft bed, you should reconsider taking a two-week tour with friends who like to stop for pictures at every vista and eat rehydrated chili.

Before sacrificing any of your precious vacation, test the waters with short weekend rides together. Warning signs include breaking into uncontrollable sobbing over a third flat tire, a tendency to rechart the course around every looming hill, and pitching your bike off a cliff because the forecast calls for rain—again. If this sounds like you, either go it alone or stick to one-day rides.

■7■ FIFTEEN WAYS TO MAXIMIZE ENDURANCE

1. Drink before you're thirsty.

2. Avoid dehydration-induced fatigue by drinking before, during, and after long rides.

3. On a warm day, drink two bottles of liquid per hour.

4. Consider using an energy drink. Such a specially designed mixture will quench your thirst and supply vital glucose.

5. Eat carbohydrate-rich meals (pasta, rice, and the like) during the three days before the event. Have fruit, oatmeal, whole-grain cereal and bread for breakfast the day of the ride.

6. During the ride, eat before you're hungry. Bananas, dates, and cookies with dried fruit are excellent.

7. Eat lightly, but steadily. Stuff your pockets at rest stops, not your stomach.

8. Vary your riding position. Move your hands from the drops to the brake lever hoods to the top of the handlebar. Stand on the pedals and arch your back for relief from bent-over cycling. Do slow neck rolls and shoulder shrugs to prevent upper-body stiffness.

9. Divide the ride into segments and prepare a strategy for each.

10. If fatigue sets in, don't dwell on the miles remaining. Instead, concentrate on form, efficiency of motion, and drinking and eating adequately.

11. Rest if necessary, but don't stop for more than 10 minutes. Longer breaks will make you stiff and sap your motivation.

12. Make sure your bike is properly geared for the course. Ask the ride organizer or someone who has ridden the route before for advice.

13. Wear cycling shoes that fit comfortably, cycling shorts with a chamois, and well-padded cycling gloves. Sunglasses protect the eyes and reduce fatigue from glare.

14. Ride with a friend who has a similar time goal. The companionship and conversation will help the miles pass quickly.

15. When the going gets tough, take a tip from Race Across America veteran Michael Shermer and tell yourself, "I can do it. Thousands of other cyclists have faced these same difficulties, and they overcame them. I can succeed, too."

8 MAKING EVERY RIDE GREAT

You know you're having a bad ride when: (a) you're going so slow that dogs don't bother chasing you; (b) before the first hill you already have three excuses for taking a shortcut home; (c) you're slightly envious of passing motorcyclists; (d) all of the above.

Every cyclist has an occasional bad ride: those inexplicable, frustrating days when your legs feel heavy and your lungs seem two sizes too small. Actually, each time you get on your bike, several factors collaborate to make the ride either enjoyable or miserable. The most important are training, nutrition, and mechanics. Most of the advice we've given so far focuses on these three crucial areas. But now we'll examine everything else, specifically the many lifestyle and environmental factors that influence riding. These range from how well you've been sleeping to whether you drank a few beers the night before, plus the amount of personal stress you're under; the scenery, weather, and terrain; your health; your familiarity with the route; how much coffee you drank at breakfast; and whether you're riding by yourself or with a friend.

We tracked a group of fast recreational riders and racers for more than a year. Periodically, they were asked to rate specific rides and answer a series of questions concerning the factors influencing them. In all, 68 percent of the rides received positive ratings, 32 percent negative. In comparing the factors surrounding good and bad rides, several trends emerged. By applying these findings—as well as the latest scientific research— you'll be able to minimize your bad days on the bike and make almost every ride a great one.

Alcohol

Two-thirds of Americans drink alcohol—and plenty of it. In fact, the average beer drinker downs 350 cans a year. According to a study conducted by the U.S. Navy, all this carousing has a lingering effect on performance. Researchers found that one night's sleep isn't enough to return you to prior levels. Thus, if you party hard on Friday night, don't expect to ride well again until Sunday.

Alcohol hurts performance by disturbing your body's delicate balance of iron and other vital elements, according to a Soviet study. It also causes you to lose a great deal of water. In fact, your body needs 8 ounces of water to metabolize 1 ounce of alcohol. So, ironically, even though you're drinking large amounts, you can dehydrate. In our survey, more than half of those reporting a bad ride had drunk alcohol the night before.

As for other forms of partying, marijuana and cocaine use can also lead to a bad ride. One Canadian study showed that smoking pot before cycling causes a significant drop in maximal work capacity and overall performance. Marijuana also impairs perception, mental functioning, muscle strength, and balance.

While there are no human studies detailing the effects of cocaine on exercise, research with animals indicates that it may have an adverse effect. In addition to increasing heart rate, cocaine stimulates the central nervous system, thus masking the onset of fatigue and encouraging overwork and possible injury. It can also cause personality change, deterioration of work habits, addiction, and, in large doses, death.

Sleep

Studies show that the amount of sleep you get affects physical capabilities less than you might think. Strength, reaction time, aerobic ability, and heart rate don't change significantly even after 60 hours of sleep deprivation. What does change is mood and perception. On long rides, these can inhibit performance. Thus, the main effect of insufficient sleep is psychological.

This was perfectly demonstrated during John Marino's cross-country record attempt in 1978. Marino's crew sped him across the United States by telling him he was sleeping 6 hours a night. After such long, restful sessions, he would take to the road with renewed urgency and vigor. It wasn't until he was almost to the finish that he realized his crew had deceived him. He had gotten only 2 hours of sleep per session. But the trick had worked. Fooled into thinking he was well rested, Marino set a transcontinental record of 13 days, 1 hour, and 20 minutes.

Although it's pretty hard to fool yourself about how rested you are, there are other ways to ensure mental freshness. For instance, take a daily nap if possible. It's been shown that regularly scheduled naps bolster performance more effectively than napping only to make up for lost sleep. Also, to improve the quality of your sleep, ride early in the day rather than in the evening. This way, the energy created by the ride will carry over into your daily activities rather than your rest time. And forget the old athlete's axiom that the most important sleep comes two nights before a big event. There's no evidence to support this. Other tips include avoiding sleeping pills (they deprive you of needed dream sleep) and taking a warm bath before bedtime (it facilitates deep sleep). In addition, being fit also results in healthier sleep patterns.

In our survey, good rides were generally preceded by an average of 8 hours of sleep, the bad ones by less. There's no magic number, however. How much sleep each individual needs is largely determined by genetics. Interestingly, 13 percent of the cyclists enjoying good rides reported that they hadn't been sleeping well lately.

The bottom line: Never lie in bed worrying about sleep. It affects you only as much as you let it.

Career and Family

A bad day at home or the office can often become a bad day on the road. Likewise, when things are going well with your personal life or career, you often feel better on the bike.

"If you're like the majority of people, your riding will be affected by what's going on in your life," says Michael Shermer, a sports psychologist and cyclist from La Canada, California. "For instance, if the problem in your home life is that your spouse thinks you're spending too much time on the bike, this can bring guilt, which can ruin your ride. However, there are certain people who can have a great ride no matter how bad things are in their life. For these people, it's an escape. They let out their pent-up frustrations by riding."

Adopting such an escapist attitude isn't easy, however. Fortunately, there are other options. If your job is stressful, try commuting to work by bicycle so you're more relaxed to start the day. If your home life is a problem, try getting your spouse or other family members interested in the sport. Such creative measures may be necessary for the health of your career, your relationship, and your riding. A recent study indicated that you're more likely to stay interested in the sport if your spouse is a cyclist, too.

Caffeine

For thousands of years, humans have used caffeine as a stimulant. Derived from any of 60 plant species, this natural compound boosts the central nervous system. And for cyclists, there's an added benefit: Caffeine spares carbohydrate stores.

These stores, known as glycogen, provide the most efficient fuel for endurance exercise. But your glycogen stores are limited, and when they're exhausted after several hours of riding, you slow down. Caffeine releases fatty acids into the bloodstream, thus promoting the use of fat as a fuel. This spares the glycogen and allows you to exercise longer. Many studies have confirmed caffeine's ergogenic effects on cyclists. One even suggests that caffeine increases the power of leg muscle contractions. However, there are drawbacks. Caffeine can cause headaches, trembling, nervousness, increased urination, insomnia, and irritability.

New research has recently shed light on how and when to use caffeine for performance. For instance, a recent study conducted in South Africa shows that you don't need caffeine if you eat a high-carbohydrate diet. The increased blood sugar of such a diet cancels any need for glycogen sparing. Another study found that habitual caffeine users acquire a tolerance that keeps them from enjoying its endurance effects. To get the full caffeine advantage, researchers suggest abstaining for four days and then starting again. Meanwhile, a separate study found that the best time for a caffeinated drink is about 3 hours before riding.

How much caffeine you need has never been clearly determined. But most studies use about 300 milligrams to elicit a performance effect. This translates into two to three cups of coffee or five to six sodas. Used correctly, caffeine can increase your odds of having a good ride.

Health

How healthy you are has a great effect on how you ride. The average person gets two or three colds a year. During these times, it's best to stay off the bike. But if you must ride, take it easy, because viruses often travel to muscles, where they cause microscopic damage and fatigue. One study showed a 15 percent strength loss among people who recently had a virus. In some cases, this lasted as long as a month. In another study, viruses disrupted aerobic metabolism, which seriously depressed performance.

As you can see, in an endurance sport such as cycling, the effects of a cold or virus can be as devastating as an injury. And the standard remedies don't help much. Cold medication can cause drowsiness, impaired concentration, increased heart rate, and trembling. Even if you aren't sick, general fatigue can ruin a ride. According to experts, chronic sluggishness is usually caused by stress. A Colorado State University study found that relaxed, unstressed athletes have greater aerobic capacity, more speed, and less fatigue than their tense counterparts. And according to a separate study, the best way to ease tension is by exercising. Stress levels stay low for 3 hours after 40 minutes of exercise. This compares to just 20 minutes after the same amount of rest. So to have a good ride, relax. And to relax, have a good ride.

If you're a woman, one of the major stresses on your body is menstruation. Thus, women may find it difficult to relax or have a good ride during their period. While most studies show that menstruation doesn't affect maximal physical abilities, some research suggests that women athletes perform best 12 to 15 days after the menstrual flow has ended. Cycling during your period increases the odds for a subpar ride.

Environment

Lifestyle factors aren't always the primary influence on ride enjoyment. Often it's out of your hands, such as when it starts to rain precisely when you're farthest from home, or when the headwind turns just as you do. At times like these, the conditions decide your fate.

For instance, when riding in hot weather, your body produces 15 to 20 times as much heat as it would at rest. Thus, your energy is divided between keeping cool and keeping pace. Conversely, in cold weather the environment robs you of heat, forcing your body to work to stay warm. Muscles contract slower and fatigue comes quicker. Hot or cold, the result is reduced performance.

In fact, weather is often the difference between a good and bad ride. In our survey, 52 percent of the highly rated rides occurred on sunny days, while 65 percent of the poorly rated ones were in the rain or under overcast skies. Headwinds were cited as a problem by 70 percent of those having a bad ride.

Scenery, terrain, and distance also play a role. On nearly two-thirds of the highly rated rides, scenery was described as much nicer than usual. And surprisingly, hillier rides were usually rated better than flat ones. Apparently, the satisfaction of climbing outweighs the memories of the pain. Interestingly, though, bad rides tended to be longer, averaging 40 miles as compared to 30 for a typical good ride.

Another important environmental factor is who you're with. You're more likely to have an enjoyable ride when accompanied by someone of equal cycling ability. According to the survey, bad rides usually occur when you're alone or with stronger, more experienced cyclists. Indeed, riding in a group allows you to share the workload and draft while also enjoying companionship. But if you can't keep up, cycling with others can prove embarrassing, demoralizing, and exhausting.

Traffic is another major influence on riding enjoyment. In our survey, 59 percent of the bad rides took place on moderately busy streets, while 64 percent of the good rides occurred on quiet roads.

Attitude

What you're thinking before a ride influences the kind of day you'll have. For instance, nearly two-thirds of the cyclists in our survey who reported a good ride had ridden the course before.

"It has to do with visualization," explains Shermer. "I just started riding a new course and I went out with a bunch of racers who knew the route. The first time was miserable. I didn't know when a big hill might be coming. I didn't know when to rest or when to go hard. On a course you know, you anticipate everything and you're ready for it when it comes."

Give yourself time to prepare for your rides. Nearly half of the bad rides in our survey were planned less than an hour in advance. This type of spontaneous riding doesn't allow for the proper nutritional or mental preparation.

Having the right mind-set is also important. It seems

riders enjoy themselves more when they disregard the clock. Of the cyclists reporting good rides, 42 percent said they were unconcerned with speed or time. In fact, when these riders were asked what specific factors made the ride special, the most common answer was having the right attitude and expectations beforehand.

Of course, even with a positive outlook, once in a while you may still have those days when not even the dogs pay attention.

▪9▪ ALL ABOUT SADDLE SORES

This is the last thing you expected. It's the fourth day of a ten-day bicycle tour. Your equipment is working perfectly, you're feeling fit, and the weather is excellent. But you've got an almost unbearable pain in the butt.

You first noticed it when you climbed back in the saddle this morning. Now it's all you can think about. Every bump in the road reintroduces you to the sharp discomfort. After all your training and planning, your vacation has been sabotaged by a saddle sore.

A saddle sore is a crotch-area infection that commonly affects long-distance cyclists. Saddle sores are one of those things that many riders suffer from, but few talk about.

It usually begins as a small pimplelike bump on your crotch (the skin between your legs or on the lower portion of your rear end). In most cases, a saddle sore's life span is just a few days. But in this time, it may become hard, red, inflamed, and quite painful.

In some cases the infection doesn't disappear. It spreads to adjacent tissue and creates larger sores, boils, or cysts that affect more tissue and may even require surgery.

Saddle sores are caused by bacteria that live on your skin. The crotch area is a perfect breeding ground for bacteria. It's warm and moist, and the glands in the skin secrete fluid that is rich in fat and other nutrients. The result is a flourishing of several kinds of bacteria in the area.

Normally, these bacteria live harmlessly on the skin's surface. But cycling changes all this. It causes pressure and irritation at the crotch. This can force the bacteria through the skin's protective outer layers into the sensitive inner layers. Once the bacteria penetrate the skin in this way, a saddle sore usually begins to form.

When the infection occurs, your body builds an impermeable barrier around the site. Usually this seals it off from the rest of the body.

Cycling, however, interferes again. When you ride, you sit on the sore. This puts pressure on the protective barrier and may cause it to rupture. When a saddle sore bursts, its contents are spilled into the surrounding tissue and the infection spreads. If this occurs, the result can be a large boil or cyst.

Small sores don't present any immediate hazard to your health. They're simply an uncomfortable inconvenience. But if they turn into larger sores or boils, they can cause scarring and permanent skin damage. Cysts are even worse. These hard lumps are easily reinfected and often must be removed surgically, as happened to Irish pro Sean Kelly in the 1987 Tour of Spain. Because of a cyst, Kelly, who was leading the race, was forced to quit.

To prevent saddle sores, be mindful of the following:

1. Wear padded cycling shorts without underwear. The chamois in the crotch helps reduce heat and friction, thus minimizing bacterial growth.

2. Keep your shorts clean. Try to wash them after every use. It's a good idea to have at least two pairs of cycling shorts so you always have a clean pair ready.

3. Dry the shorts inside-out in the sun. Ultraviolet radiation kills bacteria.

4. Avoid wearing tight pants when not riding. By increasing air circulation and keeping the crotch area dry between rides, loose-fitting clothes help reduce bacterial growth. Sleeping without underwear may also help.

5. Wash regularly with an antibacterial soap. Stewart Pharmaceutical's "Hibiclens" and Purdue Frederic's "Betadine Surgical Scrub" work well and are available at drugstores without a prescription. Daily use of one of these products will reduce bacterial growth and your chances of developing saddle sores. (Regular soap doesn't help because it has no antibacterial agents.)

6. Check your bike. An incorrectly positioned saddle can cause chafing in the crotch area, which then becomes especially susceptible to infection. To minimize the risk, keep your saddle at the right height. (Your knee should be slightly bent at the bottom of each pedal stroke.) Also, keep it parallel to the top tube. This will ensure that you don't put undue pressure on your crotch.

If you still get a saddle sore despite these precautions, the best initial treatment is to wash the area a couple times a day with antibacterial soap and keep it as dry as possible between cleanings. You can apply talcum or baby powder before riding. This reduces friction in this area, which helps keep the sore from spreading.

Don't cover it with salves or ointments, because these may actually keep the bacteria alive. Also, don't apply alcohol. It can dry the skin and cause cracking and additional irritation that may lead to even more saddle sores.

Use a mirror to monitor the sore. If it grows, hardens, or persists for more than a few days, continue the washings and take a couple of days off the bike. If it's still there in a week, see your doctor or a dermatologist.

◼10 PERFECT POSITIONS

Are you uncomfortable on long rides? Does your upper body get stiff and inhibit the strength of your lower body? Are you blaming the bike?

Let's do an experiment. Put down this book for a minute and tense your shoulders so they're up near your ears. Then extend your arms in front of you and lock your elbows. Now clench your fists. Hold this position.

Uncomfortable, isn't it? But believe it or not, most people ride this way, and it's no wonder they have trouble completing 75 or 100 miles. The key to comfortable riding is a properly fitted bike and a natural cycling position. Here are some pointers for road and off-road riders.

A Road Rider's Guide to an Effortless Glide

Arms: The arms should be slightly bent to absorb road shock. Keep the elbows in line with the body, not splayed.

Upper body/shoulders: Overall, make your legs do as much of the work as possible, not your upper body. Even when climbing or pushing hard on the flats, keep this area relaxed. Don't hunch.

Neck: Don't keep your head in one position for a long time. Periodically tilt or roll it to either side to ease the strain on your neck.

Hands: Avoid holding the bar in a death grip. Place your hands on the drops when going fast or riding into a headwind. Grasp the brake hoods for easy-paced, flatland riding. Hold the top of the bar for added leverage and easier breathing on long, steady climbs. Change hand position frequently to avoid numbness. When standing, grasp the hoods lightly and gently rock the bike with each pedal stroke. At all times, keep the thumb and a finger closed around the hoods or bar to prevent losing control on an unexpected bump.

Handlebar: The bottom, flat portion of the handlebar should be level or pointed slightly down toward the rear hub.

Photograph 1-5. Duplicate this position on your road bike and you'll be able to ride farther and faster, more comfortably. Notice the relaxed arms, the straight back, and the placement of the knee and ball of the foot over the pedal axle.

Handlebar width should equal shoulder width. This opens the chest to facilitate breathing without creating unnecessary wind drag.

Brake levers: Wrists should be straight when grasping the levers from the handlebar drops. This is accomplished by setting lever position so their tips just touch a straightedge extended forward from under the straight portion of the bar.

Stem height: The top of the handlebar stem should be about an inch below the top of the saddle. If you can lower it a little farther without upper body or breathing discomfort, do so—it will make you more aerodynamic.

Top tube and stem length: The combined top tube and stem length should be such that the front hub is obscured by the handlebar when you're seated with hands on the brake hoods. This is a starting point, and the result should be a comfortable position with a straight back and slightly bent arms. With time, you may benefit from a more extended position (a longer stem extension). This can aid aerodynamics, enhance breathing, and straighten the back. Many riders find they can use a stem that's 1 to 2 centimeters longer as they gain experience.

Back: Whether riding on the brake hoods or the drops, the back should be straight. Sharp curves often indicate a stem and top tube combination that's too short. Try to rotate the top of your hips forward to minimize the bend in your lower back. Gradually, you'll adapt to this position.

Saddle height: The distance from the center of the bottom bracket to the top of the saddle should be 0.885 of inseam length (measured in stocking feet from floor to crotch). The knees should be slightly bent at the bottom of the pedal stroke, and, when viewed from behind, the hips should not rock in the saddle. Raise the saddle 2 or 3 millimeters if you have large feet for your height. Make all changes 1 or 2 millimeters at a time to avoid injury.

Saddle tilt: The saddle should be level or pointed slightly up at the tip. Don't tilt it down, which causes you to slide forward and place additional weight on your arms.

Frame: Frame size should be such that 4 to 5 inches of seatpost are exposed once saddle height is correct. (Frame size refers to seat tube length, generally measured from the center of the bottom bracket to the top of the top tube.) Overall, a smaller frame is desirable for lightness and stiffness. However, don't use such a small one that the top tube is too short or the seatpost must be set past its maximum extension line.

Knee-over-pedal: A plumb line dropped from the bony protrusion below the kneecap should bisect the forward pedal's axle when you're seated comfortably with the crankarms horizontal. Adjust this by moving your saddle fore or aft. You may wish to experiment. Placing the saddle 1 to 2 centimeters farther back fosters a powerful pedaling style for climbing or time trialing. Moving it 1 centimeter forward aids spinning and sprinting.

Butt: Move backward on the saddle when climbing or pushing big gears. Move forward for increased leg speed during sprints or short, hard efforts.

Feet: To prevent knee injury, cleats should be adjusted so that the angle of your foot on the pedal is natural. To visualize this, think of your footprints when you walk from a pool—some people's feet angle outward, while others are pigeon-toed. The Rotational Adjustment Device (RAD), which is part of the Fit Kit bicycle sizing system used by some shops, can help transfer your natural foot position to the bike. Also, the the widest part of each foot should be directly over the pedal axle. Be sure toe clips allow at least 5 millimeters of clearance to the tip of your shoes. If they don't, install a larger size.

Pedaling technique: Concentrate on feeling the pedal all the way around. Use your hamstrings to pull back at the bottom of each stroke. Consciously raise your knee and heel on the upstroke. This will eliminate "dead spots" where no force is being applied.

Crankarm length: The trend is toward longer cranks. These supply added leverage but may inhibit spinning. In general, if your inseam is less than 29 inches, use 165-millimeter cranks; 29 to 32 inches, 170 millimeters; 32 to 34 inches, 172.5 millimeters; and more than 34 inches, 175 millimeters. (Crank length is measured from the center of the fixing bolt to the center of the pedal mounting hole. It's usually marked on the back.)

Off-Road Stuff
for Creating Diamonds in the Rough

Arms: The arms should be comfortably bent for shock absorption. If you can only reach the bar with elbows locked, get a shorter stem and/or learn to lean forward more. If your upper arms and shoulders fatigue quickly, you may need a longer stem or a frame with a longer top tube.

Upper body: As with road riding, strive for a loose, relaxed upper body.

Hands/wrists: These should remain as relaxed as possible without sacrificing a firm grip. For most situations, holding the bar with the pinkie and ring finger is sufficient. This leaves the index and middle fingers free to operate the brakes. Keep the thumbs wrapped under the grips, not on top where a jolt could cause your hands to slip off. On rough terrain, grasp the bar firmly to transfer the shock to the arms. A light grip lets the bar vibrate against the hands, causing stinging or numbness. Although squishy foam grips feel good on the showroom floor, firmer, less compressible ones are better because they don't fatigue the hands as much.

Handlebar width: Bar width should feel comfortable and natural with your hands on the grips—21 to 24 inches is

Photograph 1-6. Strive to look like this on your mountain bike and you'll be able to handle any obstacle that arises. Note the upright riding position and the smaller frame for control and maneuverability.

common. A wider bar affords more slow-speed control, while a narrower one gives a more aerodynamic position. You can shorten the ends with a hacksaw or pipe cutter.

Handlebar sweep: Bars are also available with varying degrees of rearward sweep, from 0 to about 12 degrees. (A few have as much as 22 degrees.) Try them to determine which affords the most natural wrist position. Be aware that changing the rearward sweep also alters the reach to the grips and could necessitate a different stem extension.

Stem height and rise angle: The stem's rise angle relative to the ground and its height adjustment in the steerer should place the bar 1 to 2 inches below the top of the saddle. This shifts enough weight to the front wheel for climbing control. If you need a high-rise stem, get one—don't try to compensate by extending a too-low stem past its maximum extension mark. It could snap off or pull out.

Top tube and stem length: Top tube length and stem extension combine to govern handlebar reach. Since mountain bikes have extralong seatposts, it's often top tube length, rather than seat tube length, that's the deciding factor in whether to buy a smaller or larger frame size. The result should be comfortably bent arms and a straight back.

Back: A forward lean of at least 45 degrees is most efficient because the strong gluteus muscles of the buttocks don't contribute much when sitting more upright. This also shifts some weight to the arms, so your butt doesn't get as sore.

Saddle height: Your most efficient saddle height is the same on and off road. However, use the quick-release to lower the saddle an inch or so on rough terrain so the bike can float beneath you without pounding your crotch. On steep descents, lower the saddle even farther so you can hang off the back. This keeps your weight low and rearward, allowing the front wheel to float over surface irregularities while keeping the back tire in contact with the ground.

Seatpost: On a properly fitted mountain bike you'll see a lot more seatpost than on your road bike. That's why off-road posts are commonly 300 to 350 millimeters long. This isn't a problem as long as you don't exceed its maximum extension line.

Saddle tilt: Most off-road riders prefer a level saddle. However, some like a slight nose-down tilt to avoid irritation. Others point the nose up slightly to ease arm strain.

Frame: You need a lot of crotch clearance so you don't hurt yourself if you need to hop off. Ideally, the top tube on a mountain bike should be 2 to 4 inches lower than that of your road bike. This rule isn't critical for pavement and smooth dirt riding. However, as with road bikes, there's no advantage to riding a frame any larger than the smallest size that provides enough seat height. Moreover, smaller frames are lighter, shorter, and more maneuverable.

There are differences in how manufacturers specify mountain bike frame sizes. Some measure from the center of the bottom bracket to the center of the top tube, others to the top of the top tube, and others to the top of an extended seat lug. Plus, many mountain bikes have sloping top tubes that result in tiny seat tubes. In this situation it's possible that a 15- or 16-inch mountain bike is the ideal size for someone who rides a 23-inch road bike. (For a more valid comparison, measure bikes with a sloping top tube from the bottom bracket to the top of an imaginary horizontal top tube.) Overall, the best rule is, "When in doubt, try it out."

Knee-over-pedal: Fore/aft saddle position should *never* be used to compensate for improper handlebar reach—that's why stems come in different lengths. When you're seated comfortably, a plumb line dropped from the bony protrusion below your forward kneecap should bisect the pedal axle with the crankarms horizontal. Slide the saddle forward or back to adjust this.

Butt: When riding, don't always sit squarely in the middle of the saddle. Slide to the rear for added power or to keep the back wheel planted on a steep descent. On steep climbs, crouching over the handlebar while sitting on the saddle nose maintains traction and keeps the front wheel down.

Feet: With the ball of the foot over the pedal axle, there should be at least 5 millimeters of clearance between the shoe and the toe clip. Since mountain bike shoes are bulky, toe clips made for off-road use are correspondingly larger than road bike clips.

Pedaling technique: As with road riding, smoothness is desirable. However, a mountain bike's longer crankarms, combined with steeper climbs and rough terrain, contribute to a slower cadence. So will nonround chainrings. On rough trails, pushing a higher gear at a lower cadence allows the legs to bear most of the rider's weight, reducing abuse to the arms and butt. Take really bumpy terrain out of the saddle, crouched over the bike so it's free to move.

Crankarm length: This usually varies with frame size. For added climbing leverage, most riders use cranks that are 5 millimeters longer than those on their road bikes. (Cranks are measured from the center of the fixing bolt to the center of the pedal mounting hole, and the size is usually marked on the back.)

Other Comforting Tips

For long-distance comfort it's also essential to minimize the friction between you and the bike. It's the contact points— hands, feet, seat—that need the most attention. The first step is wearing the proper clothing.

Padded cycling gloves. They help absorb road shock. But don't be fooled into thinking that more padding is better. Lightweight gloves are less constrictive and adequate for all rides. Just be sure they fit snugly, but not so tight that circulation is reduced.

Stiff-soled cycling shoes. With cleats, they enhance pedaling efficiency and minimize foot fatigue. Fit is crucial. Unlike running shoes, there doesn't need to be extra room in the toe box. Buy a pair that fits snugly.

Bike shorts with a padded seat. Well-made shorts reduce friction in the groin area. With the proliferation of mainstream cycling clothing, be sure to buy quality shorts with a chamois liner. It's always surprising to see people on long rides wearing tennis shorts. They're making a big mistake.

Videotaping is an inexpensive and graphic way to notice deficiencies in riding form that may be detracting from your comfort. Everyone benefits from seeing themselves perform. And often, it's the subtlest change in body position that yields the greatest results. But to make that all-important correction, you have to realize what you're doing wrong—and the camera doesn't lie.

Change your position and/or riding style gradually, however. Sudden adjustments can cause injury. Reassess your progress periodically by videotaping or asking a training partner for his or her evaluation. Over the long haul, you'll be happy you did.

◼11 REACHING YOUR POTENTIAL

You've probably ridden with new cyclists who seem to take naturally to the bike. They have quick reflexes, a good sense of balance, and ample strength. In time, they might even have beaten you in a sprint or surpassed your personal best in a century. When this happened you may have started wondering just how much genetics influences performance and what effect training really has on your ability to ride fast and far.

At an exercise symposium in 1967, a renowned sports physiologist, Per-olof Astrand, made a statement that asserted the influence of genetics on athletic ability.

"I am convinced," he said, "that anyone interested in winning Olympic gold medals must select his or her parents very carefully."

Indeed, cardiopulmonary physical therapist Randy Ice, who has been testing Race Across America riders for six years, contends that 60 to 70 percent of the variance in aerobic capacity (the amount of oxygen a person is capable of gathering and processing in a given time) is genetically determined. Other researchers have estimated similar percentages for such physiological factors as anaerobic threshold, workload capacity, muscle fiber makeup, and maximum heart rate.

Such testimony lends credence to the theory of biological determinism. It asserts that our biological makeup accounts for most of the variability among us. In other words, the difference between Eddy Merckx and Pee-Wee Herman is due largely to genetic inheritance (as opposed to environmental factors such as training).

No one assumes 100 percent biological or environmental determinism, however. It's the relative influence of each that forms the controversy. Indeed, if most of our capacities were determined through inheritance, what would be the use of trying to change? In the case of cyclists, why even bother training to improve performance?

Inheritability, however, does not mean inevitability. Each of us has a long evolutionary history. We are comprised of the vestiges of those who had what it takes to survive. In Astrand's usage, our parents have been carefully chosen for us—by natural selection. We are the offspring of parents who were successful enough to reach maturity, who themselves had parents who were successful enough to leave offspring, and so on back through the ages.

But as one Darwinian scholar noted, "We are what we are because of our biology in conjunction with the environment. Dogs are friendly; if you beat and starve them, they are vicious. Scotsmen are as tall as Englishmen; if you feed them simply on oats, they are runts."

The important element is each person's range of possibilities. Psychologists call it a "genetic reaction range" or the biological parameters within which environmental conditions can take effect. For example, we all have biological limits on how fast we can ride a century—a range from lowest to highest within which performance can occur. Illustration 1-1 shows this.

Cyclist A has more genetic potential than cyclist B. But their ranges overlap, and this is where such environmental factors as nutrition, training, coaching, and desire can take effect. Cyclist A may have a higher "upper wall of potential," meaning he is genetically more gifted, but it doesn't mean he'll always beat cyclist B. If the latter performs at his best and the former at only 50 percent of potential, then the genetic component is attenuated. Inheritability of talent does not mean inevitability of success.

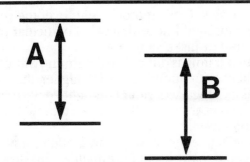

Illustration 1-1. Although cyclist A has more innate potential, cyclist B may be able to outperform him by maximizing training, nutrition, motivation, and other controllable factors.

The best way to determine your upper wall of potential is to undergo a standard set of physiological tests at a sports clinic or laboratory. In about 2 hours (and for approximately $200), you can learn your VO_2 max, anaerobic threshold, maximum workload, maximum heart rate, blood pressure, and body composition.

Knowing such values will allow you to train or amend your diet in ways that will help you realize your potential. For example, your anaerobic threshold (AT) is the point beyond which you can no longer produce energy aerobically. It's your body's breaking point during exercise. Knowing your AT (and assuming you have a heart rate monitor) allows you to train at or just below it—the most efficient conditioning range. Likewise, knowing your body-fat percentage allows you to modify your diet in ways that will make you a leaner, more efficient rider. Some labs will also do a complete blood workup, which is important in pinpointing deficiencies in overall health and training.

If $200 is beyond your budget, there are subjective ways of determining your upper limits, though none approach the accuracy and objectivity of laboratory tests. Here are a few, culled from conversations with various cycling experts.

Pete Penseyres (two-time winner of the Race Across America). "To tell you the truth, I never knew what my potential was until I had the lab tests done. I used to go on how I felt compared to previous rides. When I started riding I was always overstressed. I knew when I had passed my limits because I'd get injured or sick. I saw improvements over the years, but I'd still hit plateaus, and I never knew if a particular plateau was my upper limit or just a slow phase.

"The upper limit is difficult to determine without the tests, but invariably your limits are a lot higher than you think. When I was a Category IV rider I thought I'd never make Cat I. But within two years I was there! I don't know why I put that limitation on myself.

"My subjective test now is how I ride on my daily commute compared to my best performance. This gives me some gauge on how I'm doing. Also, if you can ride with a group that is pretty consistent in speed, you'll get a good measure of how you're doing at any particular time."

John Howard (three-time Olympic team member, Iron-

man winner, and bicycle land-speed record holder). "I use my heart rate as an indicator of when I've hit my limit. But it's not only the top end of the heart rate while riding, it's also how fast I recover and what my resting pulse is the next morning. If my resting pulse is exceptionally high, then I know I worked to my limit the day before. If my resting heart rate is ten or more beats higher than normal, then I've stressed myself.

"The lab tests are important, but the key is staying in tune with your body. I ride a 10-mile time trial every two weeks. This allows me to compare over the course of the year (and years) how my training is going. If someone wants to know their ultimate limits, they should keep pushing themselves beyond what they've previously done. This means riding with faster cyclists and getting some coaching. A coach can help push you faster, as well as teach techniques that will enable you to get past certain temporary limits."

Andy Meyers (sports psychologist at Memphis State University). "The method we use with our athletes is the Borg Perceived Exertion Scale. It's a rating from 7 to 20 based on how hard you're exerting yourself. The reason for the numbers 7 and 20 is that you multiply the exertion rating by 10 to get your heart rate. For example, a 7 would be resting in bed and a 20 would be total exhaustion. Correspondingly, for most people 70 beats per minute is their resting heart rate and 200 is their maximum. After a while you get a feel for how hard you're going and how close you are to your limit.

"As for discovering what your ultimate limits are, we have found that someone with a risk-taking personality is more likely to reach the top. By taking a risk I mean entering races, cycling with faster riders, and pushing yourself harder than before. By doing this you'll discover things about your body. We also have our athletes make a list of goals—from daily goals to dream goals—and then keep a daily log to monitor their progress toward them."

Elaine Mariolle (1986 RAAM women's champion). "I don't think lab tests are for everyone. They're a good barometer of fitness, but I'm leery about placing too much emphasis on the results. What if you're riding well and you find out you have a low VO$_2$ max? Then you get discouraged. There are too many other parameters that go into cycling.

"My philosophy is you don't just ride in order to go faster.

You should have a good time, too. Anyway, I think most people will surprise themselves with how good they can get. People told me I'd never finish RAAM, let alone win. I believe you should look forward and think positive. As for specifics, I recommend a reliable cyclecomputer that measures average miles per hour in tenths. This allows you to measure progress accurately. Compare performances over the same route. If you hit a plateau, then get a coach or find someone to help you over the hump."

Edmund Burke, Ph.D. (exercise physiologist and former adviser to the U.S. national cycling team). "Get a heart rate monitor, find a 5- to 10-mile course with no traffic lights, and do a time trial once a month. If you have a cyclecomputer, you can slowly increase your speed and watch your heart rate rise. At the point where your speed is no longer increasing and your heart rate is nearly at maximum, you will begin to hyperventilate. This is your anaerobic threshold. You should train at or just below it in order to improve speed. If you really want to increase your overall limits, cycle with better riders who force the pace."

Michael Coles (ultra-marathon cyclist). "Heart rate is very important in monitoring your conditioning and efficiency. It's analogous with the tachometer in a race car. A driver uses a tachometer to gauge the engine's performance—too low and it might stall; too high and it can burn out. The engine rpm tells the driver what level of stress the engine is at. For maximum efficiency and, therefore, the greatest possibility of winning the race, there is a medium figure below 'red line' at which you should drive.

"Likewise, a good heart rate monitor can give you a feel for your body's maximum efficiency. And I don't think it's too extravagant to have one. At first, only race cars had tachometers; now almost all cars do. If you ride alone a lot, a heart rate monitor is a great way to push yourself."

John Marino (founder of RAAM, president of the Ultra-Marathon Cycling Association, and former transcontinental record holder). "One indication of how good an athlete you potentially might be is how you did in school athletics. I remember in junior high and high school always doing well on the coach's tests of strength, speed, and endurance. So when I got good at cycling I wasn't surprised. But this may not apply to everyone, because some people may have a great potential for being an athlete without having participated in school sports. They may just now be discovering their true potential.

"I've been observing this phenomenon in ultra-marathon cycling. We have a lot of cyclists who really weren't athletes all their lives. We've opened a new segment of the sport—endurance — that is revealing potentials people never knew they had. The only way you can determine your potential is to get out and try different aspects of the sport and see where you excel. Then go for that one with everything you've got."

Randy Ice (cardiopulmonary physical therapist and president of SCOR Physical Therapy in Whittier, California). "A 25-mile time trial every so often is an excellent standard for gauging fitness. But such tests are too limiting to judge your ultimate limits. Getting the lab tests done is the only way to know for sure.

"We have to break through this mentality that sports physiology labs are for elite athletes only. They're not. They're for everyone. If cyclists are willing to plunk down $2,000 for a racing bike, why shouldn't they pay one-tenth this amount to understand the engine? As we all know, it's the cyclist, not the bike, that wins races. I'm getting people in my lab of all ages and abilities who want to understand themselves. Guessing about training went out a decade ago."

Winning Is Relative

Although the age-old debate over how much of our ability is genetically or environmentally determined, and how free we are to change these factors, may not be currently answerable, there is a compromise.

You are free to select the optimal environmental conditions that will allow you to rise to the height of your biological potentials.

In other words, you're free to work with a particular coach, free to select a nutrition program that can benefit performance, and free to direct your desire toward boosting strength and skill.

In this sense, your success as a cyclist is measured not only against others but also against the upper wall of your ability. To succeed is to have done your absolute best. To win is not just to cross the finish line first, but to cross it in the fastest time possible within your limits. The closer you come to reaching the upper wall of your potential, the greater your sense of achievement.

Part Two
NUTRITION

■12■ FOOD FOR FUEL

When you reach into your jersey for a banana during a ride, that piece of fruit begins a journey more fascinating and magical than even the greatest bicycle tour. By the end of its trip, that banana—or sandwich or cookie or whatever you ate—is transformed into energy, the key to completing *your* journey.

The way that happens is interesting indeed. Edward F. Coyle, Ph.D., a cyclist and leading carbohydrate researcher, chronicles these alterations. He lives in a fascinating world of questions: Should you eat before a ride? How can food and drink combat fatigue during a century? What type of riding is best for losing weight? How concentrated should an energy drink be? To what extent can food and drink extend endurance?

Here are some of the answers.

The Fuel of Choice

The process begins with a piece of food and the three main compounds it contains: carbohydrate, protein, and fat.

"Your body breaks down the energy stored in the molecules of the food," says Dr. Coyle, the director of the Human Performance Laboratory at the University of Texas at Austin, and a member of *Bicycling*'s fitness advisory board. "Carbohydrate is the preferred source of energy because your body can break it down faster than fat. Therefore, it rapidly releases the energy needed for a vigorous ride."

Photograph 2-1. Eating well is vitally important to the endurance bicyclist.

Fat is the body's secondary fuel source. Dietary fat is stored as an energy source, either in the blood as free fatty acids, in muscle fiber, or beneath the skin. You burn more of it on long, slow rides, which is why such efforts are often recommended for losing weight.

"When you're burning fat, you can't exercise at more than 50 to 60 percent of your aerobic capacity," says Dr. Coyle. "For instance, if you can normally maintain 24 mph, you won't be able to ride much faster than 15 mph for more than 5 to 10 minutes when you're burning fat. When you're on a fairly intense ride—maintaining a heart rate of 150 to 160 beats per minute—you only get about 40 percent of your energy from fat. The rest comes from carbohydrate. This is your body's fuel of choice." Protein is rarely used for energy, although it does play other crucial roles in the body.

How Carbohydrate Works

As it travels through your digestive system, carbohydrate—a natural compound coming from starches and sugars—is converted into glucose, a principal energy source. The glucose is then transformed into its storage form, known as glycogen. Some goes to the liver, where it's reconverted into glucose and dumped into the circulatory system. Meanwhile, other types of carbohydrate are stored in the muscles as muscle glycogen. This process, however, occurs at a much slower rate.

"Early in a ride, you rely almost exclusively upon muscle glycogen for energy," explains Dr. Coyle. "But as your muscle glycogen levels decline, you rely more on blood glucose. In just 3 hours of riding, the percentage of carbohydrate energy coming from muscle glycogen steadily declines from 100 percent to zero, while energy from blood glucose increases from zero to 100 percent."

After a few hours of pedaling without food, your glycogen and glucose stores will be depleted. Even if you have ample fat stores, the process through which these are converted to energy is not efficient enough to sustain the effort. With less fuel reaching your brain and muscles, you'll begin to feel dizzy and fatigued. Eventually, you'll run out of fuel—a condition cyclists call "the bonk."

But what if you had been ingesting carbo-rich food and liquid during the ride? Could such feedings replenish your blood glucose stores fast enough to forestall the bonk?

"Five years ago, the scientific consensus was no, carbo-hydrate feedings don't contribute significant energy for exercise," says Dr. Coyle. "The thinking was that you shouldn't bother with so-called energy drinks because they couldn't be used rapidly enough by the body. But we're finding this isn't correct.

The body can use carbohydrate during the latter stages of exercise when muscle glycogen is very low. We tested cyclists between the third and fourth hour of a ride and found they weren't using any muscle glycogen. All their carbohydrate energy was coming from the glucose they were drinking."

Dr. Coyle has shown that if cyclists eat and drink while riding, they can extend their endurance despite the fact that their muscle glycogen is exhausted. In a recent study, he had two groups of cyclists ingest either a placebo or carbohydrate prior to bonking. Those who ingested the carbohydrate were able to cycle 45 to 60 minutes longer.

"Normally, you start to fatigue and the end comes quickly. You bonk and it's over," explains Dr. Coyle. "But with steady carbohydrate feeding, you fatigue but you're still able to grind it out. The fatigue is prolonged," and the bonk is delayed.

Having determined and demonstrated the effectiveness of carbohydrate feeding, Dr. Coyle is now working to dispel some other myths.

Myth One: Experts used to believe that an energy drink should not contain more than 2.5 percent carbohydrate. It was thought that anything more would slow the solution's passage from the stomach to the intestines. This would have two negative effects. First, it would take longer for the body to absorb the fluid, which would consequently inhibit the body's ability to cool itself via sweating. Second, such slow emptying would cause nausea.

Dr. Coyle agrees that high concentrations of carbohydrate slow gastric emptying, but he disagrees with the predicted consequences.

"The stomach can empty a liter of water per hour, but it can only empty 800 milliliters per hour of a 5 percent carbohydrate solution," he explains. "Statistically, this is significant, but functionally, it doesn't constitute a big difference. No one has been able to prove that the slowdown in gastric emptying makes any difference in the body's ability to cool itself."

In fact, some recent studies have shown the opposite. Research at Ball State University compared the gastric emptying effects of ingesting 5, 6, and 7 percent solutions during a long ride. All the solutions were readily emptied from the stomach and resulted in extended performance.

Meanwhile, a University of South Carolina study compared 6 and 12 percent solutions. This one was conducted at 91-degree temperatures to gauge the effect on sweating. The 12 percent dose did not alter the body's ability to cool itself, but it *did* cause some upset stomachs.

Nausea, in fact, is the main reason extremely high concentrations are still not universally accepted. When Dr. Coyle recently fed cyclists a 10 percent carbohydrate solution, 10 percent of the subjects vomited. "When you start ingesting solutions that have 7 to 10 percent or more carbohydrate, it can build up in the stomach and cause gastric distress," he explains. "But it's very individual. Some people can tolerate any concentration and empty it quickly. The key is to experiment —find what's best for you."

Dr. Coyle explains that during exercise, the body can draw glucose from the blood at the rate of 1 gram per minute, or 60 grams per hour. Thus, to be effective, an energy drink should deliver between 40 and 60 grams of carbohydrate per hour. To accomplish this, you can either drink a little of a very concentrated solution or a lot of a diluted solution. Doing the latter will also help you meet your fluid replacement needs. However, with a 2.5 percent solution you'd have to drink several liters per hour. *Nobody* can do that.

Myth Two: Another bit of dated logic contends that eating carbo-rich foods immediately before a ride stimulates the secretion of insulin and causes fatigue. Insulin is a hormone that actually removes glucose from the blood. When combined with exercise, this can produce a dramatic drop in blood glucose, a condition called hypoglycemia. In vulnerable individuals, the symptoms include cold sweat, headache, confusion, hallucinations, convulsions, and even coma. At the very least, the shortage of glucose leads to light-headedness and lower performance. But Dr. Coyle sees it differently.

"It's overrated. Most riders never sense it," he says. "We've found that fewer than 25 percent of those who experience hypoglycemia ever have a central nervous system effect where they feel shaky or irritable. Early in a ride, it's of almost no consequence. Only 1 in 30 people notices the effects. Later, they'll notice the depletion of blood glucose because they're depriving their muscles of energy. At this point, they may be able to tolerate the effects of hypoglycemia, but they can't tolerate the fact that their legs lack energy."

By ingesting carbohydrate throughout the ride, Dr. Coyle continues, you're providing the muscles with extra energy, thus you're able to ride longer.

But why, you might wonder, can't you just keep ingesting carbohydrate and cycle indefinitely?

"Nobody knows," says Dr. Coyle. "We've studied cyclists riding with low levels of muscle glycogen but high levels of blood glucose. Their muscles seemed to be taking in glucose adequately, but after extending the exercise for about an hour, they had a second fatigue and they stopped. Something else is going on other than carbohydrate; we just don't know what."

Expert Advice

Even if science can't yet give you the ability to pedal indefinitely, you can improve your cycling performance and extend endurance significantly by using food—chiefly carbohydrate—correctly, especially on glycogen-depleting rides of 3 hours or more.

For a few days prior to an important ride, ingest 600 grams of carbohydrate per day, Dr. Coyle says. This will leave your glycogen stores full at the start of the ride.

A few hours before a ride, it's not so critical what you eat. But Dr. Coyle says to make sure that you've eaten well the previous few days, and the night before.

And during a ride?

"On any ride longer than 3 hours," Dr. Coyle says, "bring bagels, an energy drink—anything high in carbohydrate. Liquids, however, are easier to consume and provide necessary fluid. I'd suggest a carbohydrate concentration between 5 and 10 percent in volumes of 200 to 400 milliliters every 15 minutes. [A standard water bottle holds 590 ml.]"

But don't ignore solid food.

"Carbohydrate is treated the same way by your body regardless of the form it arrives in. In fact, it's good to mix solids with fluids, especially on long rides. I work with cycling teams and provide them with all types of carbohydrate fluid alternatives during races and hard rides," says Dr. Coyle. "But once they've been riding about 6 hours, they all say the same thing: 'I want something solid.' "

Next time, offer a banana, and let the real ride begin.

13 MEALS ON WHEELS

Chances are, you've always participated in sports and you've always eaten, but never at the same time. That is, until you became a cyclist. Cycling is the only sport (next to bowling) where eating and drinking are an integral part of the action. And the key factor isn't always what you eat but how you eat it. This can actually affect how well you ride.

One new rider we know discovered this during his first day-long tour. His group had covered about 25 miles in the Amish country surrounding Lancaster, Pennsylvania, when they stopped for lunch at a "family style" restaurant. To the Pennsylvania Dutch, family style means heaping bowls of ham loaf, fried chicken, roast beef, mashed potatoes, cottage cheese, apple butter, and cracker pudding, all passed from one person to the next across a communal table.

True to the restaurant's name, the food was good, and he ate plenty, but waddling back to his bike it was obvious he was dreading the remaining miles. What was supposed to be a pit stop had become a pig-out. He had made a terrible mistake.

Phillip Harvey, Ph.D., a California nutritionist and cyclist, explains that "if too much food gets into your system too quickly, your digestive system has to compete against your muscles for blood."

In our new rider's case, this translated into an overloaded body that couldn't provide enough energy for hard riding while digesting gobs of cracker pudding. Nevertheless, on any ride longer than 2 to 3 hours, you need to eat. Your body stores carbohydrate in the form of glycogen, which it later uses for muscle fuel. You have enough stored glycogen to provide energy for short rides, but not enough to last through a couple hours of strenuous cycling. The exhaustion at the end of this eventual depletion of fuel is what cyclists call "the bonk."

According to Dr. Harvey, the best way to avoid the bonk is to constantly nibble while you ride. This means eating before you're hungry and drinking before you're thirsty to keep your energy level high and your body well hydrated. For long rides, it's recommended you eat about 1 hour before leaving, then an hour into the ride, and steadily thereafter.

Just as important as when you eat is how you eat. Lon Haldeman, two-time winner of the Race Across America, says, "Some people eat [while riding] no-handed, but I've never felt comfortable doing it. If it's food that won't melt, I'll keep it in my jersey pocket and just reach back and eat it one-handed. The more fatigued I get, the less I trust my judgment. Especially late in a ride, I'll always keep at least one hand on the bar [positioned near the stem for best control].

"Rolling terrain is the hardest place to eat," Haldeman continues. "You're either flying down a hill at 40 mph and it's not safe to have less than two hands on the bar, or you're on an uphill and climbing out of the saddle. If I know I'm coming to a long hilly stretch, I'll eat ahead of time." (To reduce the risk of stomach discomfort, try to eat at least 30 minutes before a long climb starts.)

Of course, what you put in your stomach is also important. Haldeman and 1986 RAAM winner Pete Penseyres used a high-carbohydrate liquid diet to set the transcontinental tandem record in May 1987. This provided a steady source of easily accessible energy while preventing mood swings, drowsiness, and variations in performance. It also prevented dehydration, a common crippler of long-distance cyclists.

Harvey says staying hydrated is of primary importance to all types of riders. He recommends drinking one bottle of water per hour, depending on the temperature and how much you perspire. You might even want to carry two bottles, one filled with water and the other with diluted fruit juice or a commercial energy drink to provide carbohydrate.

Regarding food, Harvey notes that "the average American diet is high in fat. If this is true in your case, you'll never have enough carbohydrate to keep the glycogen stores in your legs high. And there's nothing you can do about it once you're on the bike. Just as with training, your endurance capacity depends on how well you've prepared."

To ready yourself, follow the basic tenets of good nutrition by eating a high-carbohydrate, low-fat diet. Include lots of fresh vegetables, and reduce your consumption of red meat.

On the road, eat portable carbohydrate-rich foods. Harvey suggests apples, fig bars, and oranges. And if you ever wondered why cycling jerseys have a pouch in the back, Harvey offers this theory: "Bananas," he says. "Jerseys are set up perfectly for holding bananas."

Haldeman's mobile goodie list includes celery sticks, cashews, crackers, and (this sounds familiar) apples, fig bars, and bananas. "Bananas aren't hard to peel one-handed," he adds. "You just bite off the end and peel them with your teeth."

Haldeman says you know you're really proficient at eating on a bike when you can munch a granola bar despite a runny nose. "It's a mess," he says. "You're trying to chew and swallow this dry granola bar and there's no way you can get any air. You have to go about 15 seconds without breathing."

But that's better than riding all afternoon with a bellyful of ham loaf.

14 DIFFERENT RIDES, DIFFERENT DIETS

Different types of rides require different types of nutritional preparation. For example, if you eat for a century the way you would for an interval workout, you'll be in trouble. Each type of ride has its own list of nutritional do's and don'ts. Sports nutritionist Liz Applegate, Ph.D., explains the rules: how, what, and when to eat for the five most common types of rides.

Commute

Steady speed, light to moderate effort. Distance: 5 to 20 miles. Time: Less than 90 minutes.

In preparing nutritionally for a commute, you should have two goals: (1) to ride comfortably, and (2) to have enough energy left to last the day.

For morning commutes, eat a high-carbohydrate breakfast that includes fruit, cereal, skim milk, and whole-grain bread or muffins. For lunch or an afternoon snack, eat nutritional foods such as pasta, fruits, and vegetables.

But never let your commuting get in the way of maintaining a balanced diet. For example, don't purposely avoid foods rich in protein. This can lead to long-term performance problems and dangerously affect your health.

In general, allow yourself 30 to 45 minutes for digestion before you begin pedaling. Caffeine (coffee, tea, or cola) might give you that "get-up-and-go" feeling, but it's also a diuretic. Large amounts will cause your body to lose fluid and magnify the losses you'll incur anyway while riding. This lowers performance. In fact, fluid replacement should be your primary concern during a commute. Drinking about one bottle of water per hour should be sufficient unless it's extremely hot and humid.

Middle Distance

Basic training ride, moderate intensity. Distance: 15 to 50 miles. Time: 45 minutes to 3 hours.

Nutritionally, there are two dangers to avoid on training rides. The first is allowing your energy stores to become depleted, a condition known as bonking. This can happen on rides of 2 hours or more. The second is dehydration—a loss of body fluid that results in sluggishness.

You can avoid both conditions by using energy drinks. These mixtures supply carbohydrates and liquid simultaneously in a form that's quickly used by the body. Resist the temptation to rely exclusively on these drinks, however. Cyclists still need to drink water on long rides, since sweat loss outweighs the need for energy replacement. Carry two bottles—one filled with an energy drink and the other with plain water—and alternately drink from each one every 10 to 20 minutes.

In addition, never eat fatty foods prior to riding. Pastries, chocolate, and cream cheese take longer to digest and contain less readily available fuel. In fact, carbohydrates should comprise 60 to 70 percent of your daily caloric intake, especially if you ride on consecutive days. Since individual needs are different, you may want to carry a high-carbohydrate snack as well—something like the PowerBar used by 7-Eleven team riders. For a 2-hour ride, about 100 to 200 calories should be enough.

About 20 minutes before a training ride, you should also drink 8 to 20 ounces of water. This is particularly important during the summer, when you sweat more.

Intervals

Variable speed, high-intensity efforts interspersed with active recovery. Distance: 10 to 30 miles. Time: 30 minutes to 2 hours.

Interval training is the best way to become a faster cyclist. It's also a good way to sting your muscles with excess lactic acid. Intense exertion produces lactic acid within the muscles, which eventually inhibits their ability to contract. It has been theorized that certain foods, such as cranberries and prunes, work as a buffer against acid buildup and delay muscle fatigue. But there's still no evidence to support this. In fact, there's a much more important factor involved—blood which is largely responsible for flushing away metabolites like lactic acid during high-intensity workouts.

For this reason, it's crucial that your blood isn't busy in the digestive tract when you're doing intervals and need it in the muscles. To ensure this, you should allow 2 to 4 hours for digestion before an intense ride. You should also drink at least 16 ounces of water beforehand, since perspiration losses will be great.

When riding, drink water after every interval. You don't need an energy drink or food snacks on this type of ride unless your total saddle time will exceed 2 hours. If it will, drink easily processed fluids such as diluted juices or an energy drink.

Hills

More than 50 percent of the route involves climbing. Distance: 10 to 30 miles. Time: 2½ hours or less.

A hilly ride taps your carbohydrate reserves. Thus, the key is to plan ahead and eat a preride meal of about 600 calories— for instance, yogurt, a bagel, fruit, or low-fat cookies—2 to 4 hours beforehand.

If you do this and still run low on fuel, experiment with foods and liquids that are high in sugar—soda, undiluted fruit juices, and cookies. Ingest them just before riding (15 minutes or less) and the sugar will usually kick in just when your legs begin to fade.

Preride nutrition is especially important for a hilly outing, because eating on the bike is virtually impossible. You can, however, get some energy replenishment in transit: Just fill a water bottle with an energy drink and take swigs whenever you're descending or the grade softens.

After the ride, refueling is essential to ensure proper recovery after such a hard effort. Eat enough carbohydrate and drink plenty of fluid, and your glycogen stores will be nearly back to normal in 24 hours. There are supplemental carbohydrate products (Gatorlode, Carboplex, Exceed) that are specifically designed to help you refuel properly without spending all night at the dinner table.

Long Distance

Steady speed, low-to-moderate intensity. Distance: 50 to 100 miles or more. Time: 4 hours plus.

A century is one type of ride where you can't survive bad nutrition. When a cyclist fails on a long ride, it's usually due to poor eating. The key to avoiding this is good planning before, during, and after the big event.

During a century you'll probably ride slower than normal, which means you'll burn more fat for energy. Nonetheless, carbohydrate stores are still the limiting factor. Make sure yours are high by eating lots of carbo-rich foods in the days preceding the event. A tip: Stay off the bike the final day or two before the ride and your muscles will be packed with glycogen at the starting line.

Plan carefully how and what you'll eat during the ride. Most organized centuries feature snack stops. If not, carry

TABLE 2-1.

Carbohydrate Calorie Counter

Fruit

Banana—105
Pear—98
Blueberries (1 cup)—82
Apple—81
Orange—62
Raspberries (1 cup)—61
Grapes (½ cup)—57
Strawberries (1 cup)—45

Cereal

Rice Chex (1⅛ cups)—112
Cheerios (1¼ cups)—111
Corn Chex (1 cup)—111
Wheat Chex (⅔ cup)—104
Shredded Wheat with fruit
    (⅔ cup)—100

Low-Fat Cookies

Vanilla wafers (7)—130
Animal crackers (15)—120
Graham crackers (4)—120
Gingersnaps (7)—115

Fruit-Filled Cookies

Fruit bars, raisin-filled
    biscuits—53 each

Sandwich

Pita bread filled with sliced
    fruit or shredded vege-
    tables, plain or with a
    small amount of low-
    calorie dressing—165

Dried Fruit (1¼ cups)

Figs—127
Pears—118
Raisins—109
Peaches—96
Prunes—96
Apricots—78
Apples—52

Fruit Roll-Ups

1 roll (½ ounce)—50

Bagel

Plain—160 to 200

Source: Diane Drabinsky, "Carbohydrate Calorie Counter," *Bicycling,* July 1988, p. 79.

sandwiches made with moderately low-fat ingredients such as jam, honey, apple butter, and bananas. Nibble throughout the ride. Your body handles a steady intake of small food portions much better than one overload.

Forget high-fat goodies such as candy bars. These provide more fat and less carbohydrate than you need, as well as few necessary vitamins and minerals. Caffeine, in the form of soda, may provide some energy (most likely due to its sugar content), but research shows that it has less effect if you're a daily caffeine user.

Fluid replacement is crucial. Carry at least four water bottles if there are no water stops along the route. For carbo nourishment, you can rely on either solid foods or energy drinks.

Within 6 hours after your long ride, it's important that you start to replenish exhausted glycogen stores. If you plan to ride again the next day, start eating and drinking immediately to ensure proper refueling.

While a century is a great achievement—and you may want to toast yourself with a beer at ride's end—wait a few hours if you can. Alcohol can interfere with glycogen refueling and body fluid balance.

■15■ TWINKIE POWER

Nutritionists write books on the subject. Researchers conduct long, extensive studies. Magazines publish monthly columns. But in the end, sports nutrition often comes down to this: pacing the aisles of a 7-Eleven or perusing the menu board at McDonald's when you're halfway through a ride and hungry. If you can make the right choices in these situations, you may know all that's necessary about cycling nutrition.

The first thing to realize is the value of carbohydrate. As explained previously, this is your body's most effective fuel for exercise. Foods that offer a high percentage of carbohydrate are digested faster and used more efficiently than foods that are high in fat or protein. The ideal cycling food should be at least 55 percent carbohydrate and no more than 30 percent fat. With this in mind, let's take a stroll through a convenience store to evaluate some typical choices. Afterward, we'll stop at a fast-food restaurant to learn the best (and worst) selections there. Remember that these foods are not necessarily the most nutritious choices for cycling but rather the best of the available evils.

Snack items. A 2-ounce bag of potato chips offers 306 calories, but 58 percent come from fat. By comparison, a bag of tortilla chips has about the same number of total calories, but only 42 percent are from fat—better than potato chips but still not low enough.

Nuts and seeds are even worse. Split a 6-ounce can of peanuts with your riding partner and you'll each get 471 calories. A whopping 77 percent of these are fat calories, while only 13 percent are carbohydrate. Likewise, a half can of almonds translates into 270 calories, of which 80 percent are fat and 13 percent are carbohydrate. And of the 314 calories in a 2-ounce pouch of sunflower seeds, 76 percent are fat and 14 percent are carbohydrate.

The best choice is a bag of pretzels (salt-free, if possible). Unlike nuts and seeds, they aren't naturally high in fat. And unlike chips, they aren't fried. If you eat half of a 10-ounce bag of pretzel sticks, you'll get 550 calories, of which 81 percent are carbohydrate and only 6 percent are fat.

Cookies. On a long ride you can easily burn 3,000 to 5,000 calories. Thus, you need high-calorie replenishment. Cookies provide plenty of calories, but they're often the wrong kind. For instance, two chocolate chip cookies supply about 320 calories, but 41 percent of these are from fat. Two oatmeal cookies give about 300 calories, of which 38 percent fat.

Fig bars are the wisest selection. Two give you 106 calories—83 percent from carbohydrate and just 17 percent from fat. Since their calorie content is about a third lower than that of most cookies, you can have three times as many. This helps satisfy your appetite.

Candy bars. As part of an everyday diet, candy bars and other junk foods are a bad idea. Besides being fattening, they offer few nutrients.

However, during a ride, sugary foods can play an important role by providing a quick shot of carbohydrate. The trick is to get this boost without also getting a large dose of fat. This isn't easy. A Snickers bar (270 calories) contains about an equal proportion of fat and carbohydrate. The same can be said for most candy bars, except Milky Way. Of its 260 calories, 66 percent come from carbohydrate and 31 percent from fat.

Pastry. Because of their creams and fillings, most pastry items provide more fat than carbohydrate. For instance, a Hostess cake doughnut (115 calories) is 55 percent fat.

Believe it or not, the best choice in this category may be that old junk food standard, Twinkies. That's right, two of them provide 286 calories—68 percent from carbohydrate and only 26 percent from fat.

Ice cream and yogurt. While regular ice cream is extremely high in fat, some related products make pretty good cycling fuel. Of the 167 calories in an ice-cream sandwich, for instance, nearly two-thirds come from carbohydrate and only a third from fat. A Popsicle's even better. All of its 65 calories come from sugar, which is a form of carbohydrate.

But the best selection in the dairy case is yogurt. A cup of fruit-flavored, low-fat yogurt (225 calories) is 75 percent carbohydrate and only 10 percent fat. And unlike ice-cream sandwiches and Popsicles, yogurt is nutritious, providing more calcium and B vitamins.

Cold drinks. It's easy to find high-carbohydrate sources in this area. Twelve ounces of soda supply 140 to 180 calories, all of which are carbohydrate from sugar. A more nutritious alternative that's also 100 percent carbohydrate is fruit juice (180 calories per 12 ounces). But the best choice is Gatorade. Besides being totally carbohydrate, it replaces potassium and other elements lost in sweat and is designed to reach your bloodstream quickly.

Fruit. If you find a convenience store or corner market with fresh fruit, go for it. Fruit is nearly 100 percent carbohydrate and is a good provider of vitamins, minerals, and fiber. A banana provides 100 calories, an apple about 80, and an orange about 60. For endurance and nutrition, this is your best option.

Fast food. Most cyclists know that fast food is generally high in fat and low in nutrients. However, a fast-food restaurant is often the most convenient place to eat during a ride. So is it possible to refuel properly under the golden arches or at the home of the Whopper?

The answer is yes. One way is by avoiding the big-name

burger. A McDonald's Big Mac, for instance, packs 563 calories —53 percent from fat and only 28 percent from carbohydrate. In addition, avoid french fries. A regular order adds 220 calories, of which half are fat. A chocolate shake isn't as bad (383 calories, 21 percent fat). But a burger, fries, and shake total 1,150 calories—a meal that's almost half fat.

A better option is a chicken sandwich with barbecue sauce, 6 ounces of orange juice, and a carton of low-fat milk. This gives you about 625 calories—more than half from carbohydrate and only 25 percent from fat.

The best types of fast food can be found at pizza or Mexican outlets. Four slices of a 12-inch cheese pizza (653 calories) are 59 percent carbohydrate and just 17 percent fat. Likewise, at Taco Bell, a bean tostada (179 calories), an order of beans and cheese (232 calories), or a bean burrito (350 calories) are each more than 50 percent carbohydrate and less than 30 percent fat—not quite as good as Twinkies, but a fine midride meal nonetheless.

■16■ ALL ABOUT BODY FAT

In 1985, U.S. national team cyclist Susan Ehlers was strong on the flats but climbed as if her bike had a lead saddle. That winter she shed 10 pounds, and next summer she placed second in the mountainous Coors Classic.

Early in his career, U.S. pro Greg Demgen acquired the nickname "Doughboy," because of a physique that could most charitably be called "stocky." Then he lost weight: He won the 1982 national championship road race on a 45-mile solo break.

Elite cyclists come in all shapes and sizes, but they have one characteristic in common—they're lean to the point of emaciation. A male professional rider may have only 5 percent body fat—dangerously close to the 3 percent that physiologists deem essential for health. Although equally fit women generally have 5 percent more body fat because of child-bearing demands, they still score a svelte 8 to 10 percent.

"The ideal amount of body fat for an elite male rider is 6 to 9 percent and for a woman, 11 to 14 percent," says Tim Spiro,

M.D., a sportsmedicine specialist and racer from Colorado Springs, Colorado. In contrast, he says the average sedentary adult male has 20 percent body fat, while his female counterpart has 25 percent.

"You don't want to carry any more dead weight than you need," Dr. Spiro says. "Fat is essentially nonfunctional tissue in cycling."

Cyclists with a low percentage of body fat enjoy several advantages. Most obvious is better performance on the hills. Since your body is lighter, your heart and lungs don't have to work as hard during a climb. You can consequently go faster if you're racing or more comfortably if you're touring.

In addition, your VO_2 max—the measure of how efficiently your body processes oxygen—automatically increases as you lose weight. This value is expressed in "liters of oxygen per kilogram of body weight," so if you lose 5 pounds, simple math increases your potential for performance—you've got more oxygen per pound.

But be careful. Many riders overdo weight loss, figuring that if they improve by losing 10 pounds, they'll be world beaters if they can drop 10 more. Not necessarily, says Linda Crockett, an exercise physiologist and nutrition counselor in Wheat Ridge, Colorado.

Crockett warns that it's possible to impede performance and actually endanger your health by having too low a percentage of body fat, and Dr. Spiro agrees. "There's a danger that a rider can go too low," he explains. "We don't really know why, but if men get below 6 to 9 percent, we see a much higher incidence of infectious disease, such as minor colds, as well as tissue breakdown in the form of injuries."

Because fat is nature's insulation, extremely low levels also permit a rider to chill quicker. And if you're concerned about appearance, keep in mind the cadaver look isn't any more attractive than portliness.

Ways to Lose Weight

However, if you and your cycling could benefit from dropping a few pounds of fat, there is consensus on the best way to do it. And it doesn't even involve dieting. In fact, dieting alone can adversely affect your cycling performance as well as your health. Dr. Spiro cites a study of sedentary people on low-calorie diets.

"Only between 30 and 50 percent of the weight they lost was fat; the rest was muscle tissue," he explains. "On restrictive diets you tend to lose almost equal amounts of fat and lean body tissue. But with a program combining moderate exercise and a reasonable diet, you lose weight and *increase* lean body mass. Even those who exercised but didn't restrict food intake tended to lose weight while maintaining or gaining lean body mass."

Many low-mileage riders cut calories in lieu of spending time in the saddle. They figure if they can't amass world-class miles, they'll practice world-class willpower. But as we've seen, this is a mistake. To slim down properly, gradually increase your mileage. As a result, you'll burn more calories and build more muscle, and the increased muscle mass will in turn require more calories to maintain it. At the same time, change your eating habits. Dr. Spiro advises eating fewer fats.

"If you continue to eat the same amount of food each day," he says, "but make 60 to 70 percent of it carbohydrates, you've reduced your calories substantially." With more carbohydrates available for fuel, your muscles can work longer and harder, and you can train more—an ever-improving upward spiral.

However, Dr. Spiro cautions that lowering your percentage of body fat is a long-term goal. Changing your body's composition isn't something that can be done overnight or even in a few months, and some people will have a tougher time doing it than others. In fact, advocates of what's known as the "setpoint theory" argue that each person tends to gravitate to a unique percentage of body fat.

"Setpoint is a controversial area," says Crockett. "There's no proof it exists, but people who work in weight-loss programs know that something is going on."

Adds Dr. Spiro: "It's hard to prove the existence of setpoint, but there's fairly reasonable evidence that it can be changed. Someone who is obese and tends to be 30 percent fat can settle at 15 percent and maintain it after a long-term program of exercise and diet. But it has to be done gradually."

Most cyclists, however, will never approach the leanness of an elite rider, because they don't have the time to ride hundreds of calorie-devouring miles each week. "A 30-year-old recreational rider shouldn't try to get down to the body fat levels of the elite," warns Dr. Spiro. "It would involve putting in as many miles as they do—impractical for most people. Practically speaking, getting below 10 percent for a man or 15 percent for a woman is pretty tough."

One final point: the fallacy of equating calories eaten with calories used. For example, since a pound of fat contains about 3,500 calories, you may think that by reducing your calories by 500 per day and increasing your mileage so that you use another 500 (about 45 minutes of riding at 15 mph), you'll be able to lose about 2 pounds of fat per week. This is true theoretically, but in actuality it's not that simple. Dr. Spiro mentions a study of elite runners.

"Many were eating only 1,500 to 2,000 calories a day but running more than 100 miles a week. What alternate energy sources were they using to train hard for several years on what looks like a thousand-calorie-per-day deficit? The big question is, how does someone have the energy to exercise so much on so few calories? The calculations just don't jibe. There's a lot about diet and physiology that we don't understand."

Success Stories

If all this makes losing fat seem like a difficult and complex process, take heart. Plenty of riders have found cycling to be the key to weight loss. Consider these success stories.

Jim Fiegen. A strong recreational rider and masters racer from Tucson, Arizona, Fiegen says: "When I started riding about 20 miles a day at least five days a week on a consistent basis, I lost 20 pounds over a period of four to six months. I went from 185 to 165. I didn't diet. In fact, I probably ate more because I was hungry from the exercise.

"I rode because I enjoyed it, but I noticed that the weight I'd never been able to lose before just mysteriously disappeared. I'd get on the scales every couple of days and find that I'd lost another pound or two. My wife said, 'What's going on?' and I said, 'You know that bike out in the garage...?'

"The next year when I started training hard to race, I put

some weight back on, which I attributed to muscle gain. Now I'm back to 175, but I'm a lot stronger than I was then."

Susan Ehlers. Ehlers, who was 1986 U.S. Olympic Committee "Cyclist of the Year," says: "I lost about 10 pounds. I didn't have any kind of plan, really, I just quit eating so much fat. And I rode more miles—more *intense* miles.

"Probably the dietary changes were more important than the training. I tried to eat only when I was hungry. It's easy to eat when you're on the road between races and you're bored. Mainly, I just changed my cooking. I don't eat anything with cream sauce and I fix vegetables by steaming them or by using just a tiny bit of oil. I mainly use seasonings rather than oil. And the harder training seemed to increase my whole metabolism.

"Funny—I always seem to lose weight when I go to altitude. I don't know if it's my metabolism or what, because I don't change my eating habits. But if I'm in Colorado for a while I seem to lose weight.

"Mainly, [the lower weight] has helped my climbing. I just feel more powerful. But I think I'm about as light as I can get without losing strength. I always gain a little in the winter and then it comes off as the season goes along. This is a good weight for me [135 pounds] when I'm racing, but I don't think I can stay this thin all year-round."

Susan Daney. A 48-year-old tourist and century rider from Boulder, Colorado, Daney says: "The key for me is mileage. It takes riding 60 miles a day nearly every day, like on a tour. I don't lose a lot of weight unless I do over 60 miles a day, four times a week.

"Most people only ride 20 or 25 miles maybe twice a week. If I ride twice a week I don't lose a lot of weight. Maybe 100 miles a week would do it for some people, but it's probably more like 200 for me.

"You don't need to hammer. As you get older, you tend to ride more miles instead of faster miles. For most people over 40, the way to lose weight is just miles. The problem is that most people don't have the time. But if you don't ride 200 or more miles a week—for me anyway—the weight goes right back on."

Greg Demgen. Demgen, a pro racer and cycling coach

from Madison, Wisconsin, reports: "I lost weight through diet control and regimented training. I've gotten to the point where I'm about 8 percent body fat compared to probably 20 percent when I was a kid. I think it's a hereditary thing. No one in my family is really thin. My father and mother both gain weight easily.

"I had to do a lot of miles to keep my weight down, and I always had to train harder than the average rider to even look like I was a bike racer. But the weight loss enabled me to climb more comfortably.

"There are some advantages to being stocky, though. Endurance-wise, in a stage race you'll be able to go day after day and recover easier than another rider who is really skinny. It's been a toss-up with me. I always maintained a pretty good balance between being not too skinny and not too fat."

Keeping Tabs on Your Flab

Three methods are commonly used to determine percentage of body fat. However, each is an approximation, since they rely on indirect measurements. Actual body fat percentage can only be derived through an autopsy—something that would slow you down far more than too much fat.

The traditional method involves being weighed underwater. Completely submerged in a tank, subjects are weighed and the result is compared to normal scale weight using a complex formula. Because fat is more buoyant than muscle and bone, it can be calculated using Archimedes' principle. Eureka!

This process has several drawbacks, though. First, it costs $20 to $40. Second, accuracy depends on the experience and skill of the technician. Third, some people find it uncomfortable because you must exhale as much air as possible, then remain submerged while readings are taken. By the way, technicians who do this sort of thing usually possess a rather odd sense of humor—shark posters or rubber duckies in the tank seem to be standard.

If you're afraid of water (or sharks), "skinfolds are the way to go," says Crockett. In this process, a trained technician pinches your skin at three or more locations, measures the thickness of the resulting skinfold with calipers (called "pud pliers" in the trade). These readings are then plugged into one of several formulas. Quick, easy, and relatively inexpensive ($10 to $25), it's a good way to keep tabs on your flab.

There are some drawbacks, though. The formulas assume fat under the skin is proportional to internal fat stored around bodily organs. In other words, if you hoard more fat under your skin, the results will be misleading. Also, skinfold measurements are only as reliable as the person taking them. To ensure accurate readings on successive tests, Dr. Spiro recommends having each test done the same way by the same technician. You can also buy your own skin calipers (some cost as much as $250), but without the necessary expertise it is, at best, an approximation of an approximation.

A third technique involves a recent development known as electrical impedence. In this process, electrodes are attached to your foot and hand, then a mild electric current is passed between them. Percentage of fat is figured indirectly, based on the rate of electrical resistance. This method is the quickest and the least expensive ($10 to $20) of the trio. And despite a resemblance to some forms of capital punishment, it's painless.

Results can vary widely, however, depending on your state of hydration and such seemingly unimportant factors as whether your thighs are touching. According to Dr. Spiro, "Studies have shown a great variation in fat measurements done with electrical impedence. The jury is out as to whether it's a reliable, repeatable method."

To have your body fat measured using any of these methods, check local hospitals, athletic clubs, college physiology departments, and sportsmedicine clinics.

There's actually a fourth method for gauging body fat that's the easiest and least expensive of all. Stand naked in front of a full-length mirror, look carefully, and assess what you see. Do you look lean, or are there areas of pudge? Do you have the visible ribs of fitness? Can you see your stomach muscles when they're tensed? How about definition among the various muscles that comprise the quadriceps? Such an objective, visual self-appraisal may be the best way to determine if you're at your most effective weight or if you need to lose a few pounds.

Interestingly, Crockett reports that she "always makes a visual estimate before I put people in the tank, and usually I come within 1 percent. In fact, there's a new study that shows that visual estimate is actually a pretty good technique for someone who is trained in doing it."

Part Three

MAINTAIN
WHAT YOU GAIN

17 MINIMUM WORKOUTS FOR MAXIMUM FITNESS

It's crunch time at the office. There's a report due in two weeks and you'll be working 10 to 12 hours a day in order to finish it. You'll barely have time for your family, let alone riding your bike.

You're buying a new home. Every night is spent driving around with the real estate agent or analyzing expenses. Then comes the move itself—packing, unpacking, getting resettled. You'd love to get on your bike and escape, but there's just no time.

You have a new baby. Pacing the floor with a crying infant at 3:00 A.M., mired in feedings, diapers, and all that attention—you're exhausted. You begin to wonder if you'll ride again before the kid's high school graduation.

Sometimes cycling has to take a back seat to other things in your life. The previous examples illustrate that it's not always possible to ride regularly. But you don't have to lose the benefits you've worked so hard to attain. If you're able to do just two short cycling sessions a week, you can maintain your fitness without difficulty.

The Body's Memory

During the first couple of weeks of a layoff, fitness deteriorates remarkably fast, according to Edward Coyle, Ph.D., who has conducted landmark research on the effects of detraining.

"When you stop training totally, you lose various aspects of your fitness rather quickly," he explains. "A rule of thumb is that the biomechanical changes that occurred in the muscle [with training] decline in what is called a half-time of 12 days. This means that in 12 days, you'll go halfway from your trained state to the level you'd be at if you had never trained. And you'll go another half that distance between 12 and 24 days. So essentially, in the first 12 days of inactivity, you lose half of what you developed. But your decline is more gradual after that."

Remarkably, when you're not exercising, your blood volume decreases. During the first week of layoff, your blood volume drops from about 6,000 milliliters to 5,600, or approximately 7 percent. Since you're not exercising, your body needs less blood. Thus, it stops producing as many red blood cells, and, through urination, drains several hundred milliliters of liquid.

Reduced blood volume has adverse effects on your cardiovascular system. With less blood being pumped per beat, you have a lower capacity for using oxygen during exercise. In other words, your maximal oxygen uptake (VO_2 max)—a key factor in fitness—declines. But contrary to the conclusions of older studies, cardiac benefits do not disappear quickly during a layoff.

"It used to be interpreted that your heart deteriorated, that all the improvements in heart function derived from training were lost rapidly," explains Dr. Coyle. "But this isn't the case. Your heart pumps less blood not because it's deteriorating but because there's less blood to pump."

Another outdated scientific theory holds that a short layoff can erase all fitness gains. This was based on studies in which sedentary people were put on short training programs and then taken off them. They dropped back to their initial poor fitness levels rapidly, prompting researchers to conclude that even a short break from training can erase all improvement.

However, a study conducted by Dr. Coyle at the Human

Performance Laboratory at the University of Texas at Austin shows that even with a long layoff, you keep some of your fitness gains. Dr. Coyle's study dealt with relatively fit subjects, including cyclists. He had them train vigorously for six months, and then stop training for three months. Subsequent tests showed fitness levels had declined, but unlike previous findings, these subjects maintained some of their fitness.

Their maximal oxygen uptake dropped an average of 18 percent. Two other fitness indicators, heart rate and stroke volume, deteriorated slightly for the first three weeks (heart rate increased by 4 percent; stroke volume decreased by 11 percent), but did not decline further through the layoff.

Most important, these fitness levels never went as low as a control group's, which had been sedentary throughout the study. Despite the layoff, the stroke volume of the fit subjects remained 5 percent higher and maximal oxygen uptake 12 percent higher, than that of those who hadn't trained at all. It seems the body, like the mind, possesses a memory. And once your body is trained, even three months away from the bike won't make it forget.

Minimum Maintenance

If your training will be on hold for more than a couple of weeks, however, you'll need to embark on a minimum maintenance program to keep from regressing.

"The key is intensity of exercise," says Dr. Coyle. "What you need to do is train hard at least two days a week. This maintains your maximal oxygen uptake and your ability to perform all-out efforts of up to 6 to 8 minutes."

Dr. Coyle recommends interval training. After a 20-minute warm-up, ride hard for 5 minutes, then shift to an easier gear and "rest" for 5 minutes (maintaining a 90 to 110 rpm cadence). Repeat this four more times, and end the workout with a 20-minute cool-down. Each workout will take 90 minutes. Thus, you'll have to spend just 3 hours on your bike each week to maintain your ability to ride at high intensities.

Of course, such a maintenance program is no panacea. Three hours a week won't, for example, sustain your endurance for century rides. Dr. Coyle explains: "Your ability to perform longer-duration events will decline, but not as much as you might think, and certainly not as much as if you did nothing at all. The important thing is that with reduced training you maintain intensity.

"You can reduce the number of days per week and the number of minutes per day that you ride, but you have to maintain the intensity with which you are doing the workout to maintain your VO_2 max. If you just train easily, even though you might do it frequently, you won't be as well off."

Actually, the biggest drawback of a layoff isn't losing fitness but losing the opportunity to improve it. Craig Campbell, U.S. junior national coach, contends "the longer you're away from riding, the more ground you're losing to others. If you're used to riding five days each week and you drop to two, it's easy to maintain that level of fitness—but your friends aren't maintaining, they're building."

The Layoff Advantage

The only time a layoff can help is if you've been overdoing your cycling. In this case, the time constraints of a job, a new home, or a baby may actually help you improve.

"When you're forced into a break, you often come back fresher," explains Campbell. "Maybe you've been overtraining, stressing your body, never resting completely—so you're not building as much as you could be. A break can bring you back."

Adds Dr. Coyle: "If you've been doing a lot of long rides, you may actually increase your power after a week or so of inactivity because of the rest."

Several elite racers have benefited from forced layoffs. In April 1982, Greg LeMond broke his collarbone and was out of action for six weeks. Three months later, he became the first American to win a medal in the world professional road championship. Similarly, U.S. pro Ron Kiefel broke his arm in the 1983 Tour of Texas. Later that summer, he won three national championships.

But after years of training you develop a reservoir of endurance that can't be drained by a short layoff. In fact, on

Photograph 3-1. Taking a break can actually *improve* your performance.

occasion, the rest can do you good. "Sometimes a layoff isn't as bad as it seems," says Campbell.

Still, layoffs are monotonous times. Try to do something every day, even if it's just a few calisthenics or 20 to 30 minutes on an indoor resistance trainer. Eventually, your schedule will get back to normal and you'll get back in the saddle. In the meantime, it's easy to lose what you've earned. It's also pretty easy to maintain it. The choice is yours.

 TOTAL FITNESS

"I really got into cycling last summer," said Steve, "and by fall I was in the best shape of my life. I did three centuries in three weeks and then broke my 10-mile time trial record. In the winter I played basketball and thought I'd run circles around everyone. But in my first game I was terrible. I couldn't jump, my reflexes were shot, and my legs were so sore afterward I could hardly walk for three days."

Steve, who didn't want his last name used because he was too embarrassed, had learned a difficult but vital lesson—fitness is specific to the activity that's used to develop it.

Stated another way, being fit for cycling doesn't necessarily mean you're totally fit. Pro road riders are often called the fittest athletes in the world because of their ability to compete for up to 8 hours each day in three-week-long stage races such as the Tour de France. Yet many top roadies have a notoriously weak upper body and lack the hand-eye coordination necessary for other sports. Off the bike, they often lack quickness, agility, and kinesthetic sense. Watching America's best cyclists play basketball at the Olympic Training Center (OTC) isn't an aesthetic experience at all.

Of course, world-class cyclists are willing to forgo all-around fitness for the specific skills needed to succeed in their particular sport. But for fast recreational riders, tourists, and weekend racers, one-dimensional fitness isn't enough. You want to be strong on the bike without sacrificing overall fitness—you want cycling to be the main course in a fitness feast, but you're not about to pass on the hors d'oeuvres. The big question: How can you do that?

The first step is to look at the components of fitness, ranked here in reverse order of importance to cyclists.

Last on the list is *agility.* Elite cyclists must be good bike handlers, but they often lack agility in other situations. To remedy this deficiency, cyclists attending OTC training camps do a progressive warm-up that includes tumbling, somersaults and gymnastics, says Craig Campbell, U.S. junior national coach.

But according to Christine Wells, Ph.D., of Arizona State University's health and physical education department, "you develop agility on the bike by riding." But she cautions that agility is "more of a motor performance thing . . . you either have it or you don't." For these reasons, off-bike agility, while certainly an advantage, is a low priority when workout time is limited.

Another skill that's desirable but not crucial to cycling performance is *hand-eye coordination.* Cycling rarely demands this skill except when a training partner tosses a water bottle to you in midride or when you try to snag a musette bag in the feed zone during a long race.

Explosive power is vital to sports like basketball and shot-putting. Cycling, however, doesn't reward one-repetition explosiveness. Endurance is more important. Even natural sprinters such as Davis Phinney distribute power over a specified distance.

Flexibility is much more important. It's essential for comfortable cycling, although the activity itself doesn't encourage it, since your legs move in a rigidly patterned circle. As a result, hamstrings, hip flexors, and other leg muscles become accustomed to an extremely limited range of motion. And chances are you'll pull muscles if you fall or chase a thief making off with your bike.

"Flexibility exercises are especially important for hamstring muscles because they're never fully extended in cycling," Dr. Wells says. In fact, tight hamstrings are often the source of back ailments. To protect yourself, adopt a stretching program such as the one outlined by Olympic champion Mark Gorski in chapter 3.

Poor *upper-body strength* is the Achilles' heel of cyclists. It's a three-pronged problem, since you need strong upper-body muscles to stabilize your position on the bike, to pull on the handlebar when sprinting or climbing, and to protect yourself in case of a fall. Ironically, cycling doesn't readily build the arm and shoulder strength it so often demands. Weight training is necessary.

Another reason to head for the weight room is simply to balance yourself physically. Too many cyclists look like *Tyrannosaurus rex,* their bulging legs topped by an emaciated upper body and scrawny arms. Keep in mind, however, that cycling performance can be compromised by an upper body that's too well developed—more muscle means more weight to carry.

Aerobic power is the ability to perform submaximal exercise for long periods. No problem here: Aerobic endurance is cycling's forte. Nevertheless, cycling is so specific to the quadriceps that sometimes other sports (such as swimming) that develop cardiovascular endurance via other muscles can be beneficial. These sports also offer a psychological break from cycling.

Your Total Fitness Program

Perhaps, in spite of the previous discussion, you're unconvinced of the importance of being totally fit. Why should you develop athletic skills that cycling itself doesn't build—and sometimes doesn't require?

The answers lie in the basic philosophy of athletics. While better hand-eye coordination or more explosive power may not be required in cycling, they help—and nine times out of ten, the better all-around athlete will win any head-to-head competition regardless of the sport. The greatest cyclists are not just bike riders but gifted athletes who've chosen cycling as their sport. And even if you don't aspire to world-class cycling status, becoming totally fit will make your riding and other athletic activities much more enjoyable.

Unfortunately, building all-around fitness takes time and energy that most riders would rather devote to cycling. But there are ways to save on both. Other aerobic sports such as rowing and swimming, for example, should be scheduled once or twice a week in place of the day's cycling workout.

Less important components of total fitness, such as hand-eye coordination and agility, should be improved by participating in a fun sport such as basketball or soccer once a week. And strength training, despite its importance, shouldn't detract from cycling. Fifteen minutes of upper-body exercises after every ride is ideal. Such an arrangement saves on warm-up time and will also put you in the proper mood for an effective weight workout.

But be careful: Don't train too intensely. Traditional weight-lifting programs involve hard training interspersed with total rest days. This won't work for you, since your hard days have to come on the bike. Thus, your weekly weight training should be divided among several short sessions in which you work different upper-body muscles.

"Cyclists don't need to be overly strong, but they do need

good supporting musculature to prevent fatigue on long rides," says Dr. Wells. The best general program to meet this goal, she continues, features 15 to 30 repetitions done with moderate weight. This builds muscular endurance and just enough muscle size to balance leg development.

Remember, however, that muscle size is hereditary—two people on the same program may get entirely different results. Also, if you're a beginner, get an experienced lifter to show you proper form for each exercise, or borrow a book on weight lifting from the library. Correct form is safe form. Save squats and other leg work for the off-season—your legs get plenty of work on the bike.

Because time is always crucial, try to do these workouts at home. Use the money you save from not joining a health club to buy basic equipment like a pull-up bar, a bench, and a 110-pound barbell set.

Here's a sample weekly schedule that mixes riding and weight training with other sports for total fitness and better cycling performance. Make sure to start and end each session—whether on a bike, on the ball field, or in the weight room—with 10 to 15 minutes of light stretching. This will promote flexibility and protect you from injury.

Monday

Cycling: Easy spin to recover from Sunday's long ride or race.

Total fitness workout: Concentrate on the pulling muscles in your upper body with one to three sets (15 to 30 reps apiece) of pull-ups, upright rows, and bent rows. If you can't do many pull-ups, stand on a chair and do the exercise using less than total body weight.

Complete the workout with a set of crunches for the abdominal muscles. To do this exercise, lie on your back and put your legs against a wall or on a bench. Curl your shoulders several inches off the floor, hold for a second or two, lower, and repeat. Dr. Wells advises against doing sit-ups because they develop the hip flexors instead of the abdominals and can aggravate a back problem. Add wrestlers' bridges for neck strength.

Tuesday

Cycling: Ride 60 to 90 minutes at a steady pace. Include some anaerobic threshold work such as sprinting or brisk climbing.

Total fitness workout: Concentrate on the pushing muscles in your upper body with one to three sets (15 to 30 reps each) of bench presses, incline presses, and behind-the-neck presses.

Wednesday

Cycling: Day off.

Total fitness workout: Use the time you would normally spend riding to participate in a complementary sport such as rowing or swimming.

Thursday

Cycling: Ride 60 to 90 minutes and include intervals or hard climbing.

Total fitness workout: Do a short upper-body workout using the military press, bent row, and bench press. One to three sets of each (15 to 30 reps apiece) is enough. End the workout with a set of back extensions, crunches, and wrestlers' bridges.

Friday

Cycling: Day off. Clean and prepare your bike for weekend rides.

Total fitness workout: Day off.

Saturday

Cycling: Do an easy hour-long ride, preferably with friends. Test the bike for the next day's long ride.

Total fitness workout: Warm up with stretching, crunches, and neck bridges. Participate in a sport that demands hand-eye coordination, quickness, and agility. It could be the same as what you did on Wednesday or something different—gymnastics, basketball, soccer, handball, or tennis.

Sunday

Cycling: Today is the highlight of the week. Go for a long solo ride, join a group ride, race, or challenge yourself with a century.

Total fitness workout: Your cycling workout is stressful enough. When you come back from the ride, do some easy stretching, take a hot shower, and relax—you've earned it.

19 A WINTER TRAINING PROGRAM

Time has been the subject of man's deepest reflections and most mundane cliches. But for the cyclist trying to squeeze maximum improvement out of limited opportunities to train, one thing's certain—there's never enough.

Some riders have plenty of time. Professionals do little else but eat, sleep, and ride. But for most riders, cycling is a hobby sandwiched between the strident demands of career and family. If you tried to emulate the pros, you'd burn out quickly. In fact, Greg LeMond says that for riders with jobs and other responsibilities, "10 to 12 hours a week on the bike is a lot."

In winter, when bad weather and short days further constrict your riding, time becomes even more precious. Winter layoffs can destroy the fitness built last summer. After a week or two off the bike LeMond says he "couldn't even finish a professional race." Studies prove that after about one month of inactivity, even the best-conditioned athletes lose most of their fitness.

So here's the challenge—emerge from winter with your hard-won fitness not only intact but improved, and do it on 6 hours a week. To make it tougher, let's assume you can't exercise two days a week. All you have to work with are four days when you can spare 1 hour, and a fifth day when you can spare 2 hours. Because your time is limited, you can't waste it commuting to a health club. All your workouts must be done at or near your home.

As impossible as it seems, there is a way to maintain and improve your fitness even given these kinds of time constraints.

Three Caveats

1. Goals. Know what you want to accomplish before you start. For instance, maybe you'd like to keep from gaining weight or perhaps lose some excess poundage. This would mean devoting a substantial portion of your winter training program to calorie-burning aerobic activities. At the same time, you wouldn't want to sacrifice any of your strength or cardiovascular capacity, so weight training and even hill running might be in order.

Whatever your goals, remember that psychologically as much as physically, you need a break from cycling. Experiment with other sports, but don't waste time on activities that won't help you reach your goals.

2. Schedule. Assess your schedule to determine, realistically, when you can exercise. If you have a long lunch hour, you might be able to ride outside on mild winter days. If you don't have any free time until late afternoon, you may have to resort to a stationary bicycle. Don't try to squeeze in workouts when time is too tight. This only leads to frustration.

3. Simplicity. Keep it simple. You're not training for the Tour de France, and your program doesn't have to be that serious or complicated. In fact, on such a limited time budget, the simpler it is, the better.

Four Essential Components

1. Cycling. During the winter, deemphasize cycling—you'll be that much more eager and enthused about it come spring. But if you neglect the bike completely you'll acquire weak legs, a tender rear end, and an ungainly pedal stroke. The trick is to ride just enough to maintain your cycling fitness. In the dark days of winter this means riding an indoor resistance trainer—the infamous stationary bicycle. With one of these handy gadgets, you can pedal inside where it's warm and dry.

But even the most dedicated riders often find an hour of indoor cycling, day after day for three months, tremendously tedious. The key to beating boredom is to use the trainer for warming up and cooling down from other activities such as weight training or running. This approach not only gives you the benefits of working at a number of different sports, it also keeps your cycling muscles in shape and affords you that all-important psychological break from riding.

Photograph 3-2. Riding rollers enables year-round weatherproof training.

Of course, if you can get out on the road, do it. But ride at a moderate-to-leisurely pace (preferably with friends) and set a goal of having fun. If the sun is out but the roads are messy, try riding a mountain bike with fenders. The knobby tires provide good traction, and their higher rolling resistance will give you an ample workout even at slower speeds.

Take that mountain bike off-road, too. You can improve your bike-handling skills, build power, and refresh yourself by tackling park paths, dirt roads, and hiking trails.

"It's great to power up the hills, get a little anaerobic, dismount, and run a little to use some different muscles," LeMond notes.

2. Resistance training. Cyclists need strong upper bodies to stabilize their riding position and prevent fatigue on extended treks. But riding by itself won't develop this type of torso. Resistance training is necessary, and winter is the ideal time to get strong.

In keeping with our ground rules, here's what you'll need to start an at-home winter weight training program.

1. An indoor resistance trainer
2. A pull-up bar
3. An inexpensive barbell set totaling 110 pounds
4. A sturdy bench

Begin each workout with a 15-minute warm-up on the stationary bicycle. Then do the following exercises. Choose a light weight—one that allows you to perform 10 to 20 repetitions without a helper. Begin with one set for each exercise. Add a second set as you get stronger, and add more weight after you exceed 20 reps. If you're inexperienced in weight training, consult a book that shows how to do the different exercises correctly, or better yet, get professional instruction at a health club.

Pull-up. Pity the poor pull-up. In this day of fancy fitness machines, the pull-up is passé. That's too bad, because it's still one of the best overall upper-body exercises for cyclists. It's important because it works the muscles that pull on the handlebar while sprinting or climbing. You can derive more benefit from the simple pull-up by varying your grip on different sets—palms away, palms facing, narrow grip, wide grip. If you're a real Tarzan and can do more than 20, tie a barbell plate to your waist for added resistance.

Bench press. This basic upper-body exercise strengthens the muscles that support your torso while riding. If your arms and shoulders ache during long rides, then you need a winter of benches. But don't aim for massive poundage. Use a moderate weight, and concentrate on maintaining good form and using your full range of motion.

Upright rowing. This exercise is the first installment of your winter insurance policy. It develops the trapezius muscles that help protect your neck in case of a fall. It also strengthens your shoulder girdle, thus guarding against collarbone fractures and shoulder separations. As a bonus, the added strength you'll derive from doing upright rows will help support the weight of your head and helmet on long rides, discouraging neck fatigue. Use light weights for this one, and don't cheat. Keep your upper body still.

Neck bridge. Here's the other half of that insurance policy. This exercise strengthens your neck so it can better withstand the shock of a potentially dangerous fall.

Push-up. This is another vital but unglamorous exercise. Push-ups strengthen your triceps, the arm muscles that help stabilize your upper body, especially during long stints on the drops. Push-ups are a good supplement to bench presses because they work the same muscles at a different angle. As with pull-ups, vary hand spacing. Or try doing them with your feet elevated on a bench.

Squat. This is the best exercise for developing leg power because it works your quadriceps, hips, and lower back—the same muscles that produce your pedal stroke. Sometimes maligned as a cause of injury, squats are safe if you follow three rules.

- Use light weights and do high repetitions (15 to 30).
- Squat until the tops of your thighs are parallel to the floor. Don't go lower unless you're experienced doing full squats.
- Maintain correct form. Keep your back flat, your head up, and your chest out. Don't bounce at the bottom of the movement.

Crunch. This exercise builds strong abdominals. While these muscles aren't used in cycling, they are crucial for supporting and aligning your back.

End your workout by cooling down on the resistance trainer.

3. Aerobic activities. For variety and well-rounded cardiovascular development, cyclists should participate in other aerobic activities during the winter.

Running is especially useful in the off-season. It's not only possible to run under adverse conditions, it's also feasible to get a good workout in a relatively short period of time. In addition, running strengthens the calves and hamstrings—two areas that cycling overlooks. Hard uphill running taxes the cycling muscles.

Running has its disadvantages—chiefly the possibility of injury. To avoid being sidelined, invest in quality shoes with good support. On downhills, run slowly or walk. And most important, start your running program gradually. You might start by running 5 miles this way: walk 2, run 1, and walk the last 2. Each time out, increase the running segment of the workout by a half mile until you're running the full 5 miles without stopping.

If you have access to a pool and the time to use it, swimming is one of the best total body conditioners. You'll develop upper-body strength and flexibility as well as cardiovascular power.

Cross-country skiing is another great endurance activity. In fact, the poling motion affords the same benefits as spending an equal amount of time in the weight room. If you're skeptical, just wait until you feel those tender triceps the morning after. And according to Don Christman, a cyclist and ski coach at Western State College in Colorado, "The newer skating technique works cycling muscles more than the older diagonal stride."

LeMond, an avid skier, has this to say: "If you did a good ski program for three months [in the winter] and rode an ergometer two or three times a week, you'd be ready to race with only three weeks of road training at the beginning of the season."

A final off-season conditioner to consider is aerobic dance.

Even if you don't have the time to go to a health club, you can simply turn on the tunes and do some exercises. Invite someone over to share in the sweat. Or try alternating each of a dozen exercises with 1-minute bouts on the resistance trainer, all accompanied by raucous rock.

4. Other sports. No winter program is complete without including some fun sports to hone coordination and agility. Try the old standbys: basketball, volleyball, soccer, handball, and racquetball. Or go for more exotic activities like gymnastics, or snow tag with the kids. The more time you spend riding your bike in the summer, the more your basic coordination and agility tend to deteriorate. Retain and rebuild your ability to walk and chew gum at the same time by participating in active sports in the winter.

Building a Workout Schedule

Here's a sample workout schedule for a cyclist who works from 9:00 A.M. to 5:00 P.M. and has family responsibilities. In keeping with the ground rules, he or she has just 6 hours a week to exercise. This includes 1 hour three days a week after work when it's too dark to ride outside, another hour on Saturday morning, and 2 hours on Sunday.

Monday: Rest.

Tuesday: Spend 30 to 45 minutes running, skiing, or doing some other type of aerobic activity. For the rest of the hour, ride the resistance trainer at a moderate pace.

Wednesday: Warm up for 15 minutes on the trainer. Do resistance exercises for 30 minutes. Then cool down on the trainer for another 15 minutes.

Thursday: Warm up with light stretching, jogging, or spinning on the trainer. Then participate in an active sport such as basketball. Cool down on the trainer.

Friday: Rest.

Saturday: Do any aerobic activity for 45 minutes, followed by 15 minutes of resistance exercises. If the weather cooperates, ride your bike.

Sunday: If the weather stays nice, ride for 2 hours at a moderate pace. In poor weather, combine activities. For instance, run for 30 minutes, do aerobics for 30 more, ride the windtrainer for 45, then stretch and do calisthenics for the remaining 15.

As the weather improves and the days get longer, devote more time during each weekday workout to cycling and start adding miles to your Sunday ride. You'll be ready for group rides, tours, centuries, and club races in no time.

Proof That It Works

If you're still unconvinced that 6 hours a week is all you need to ensure yourself a great fitness base next season, consider Jeff Little, a 37-year-old rider from Hanover, Pennsylvania. In 1987, he completed a 300-mile ride in less than 20 hours despite having his training time limited by family responsibilities and a full-time job in retail management. How did he do it? "I trained for 30 weeks averaging 6½ hours a week overall," he reports.

It can be done. And such an abbreviated schedule offers another important advantage—it lets you rest. Cyclists with a limited amount of time to train must be even more aware of chronic fatigue and overtraining than full-time racers. If you compare your summertime peak of 100 or 150 miles a week to LeMond's 600, you're apt to think you can't be overtraining, no matter how tired you feel. But LeMond rides 4 to 5 hours, gets a massage, eats meals arranged by his team manager, and has a mechanic to clean and adjust his bike. Conversely, you train for 1 or 2 hours, work for 8 or 9, run errands all over town, go watch your child play baseball, and plan the household budget with your wife. Plus, there's no mechanic taking care of your bike. Your stress load is much greater than that of a pro who rides four times your mileage.

Given such circumstances, a shortage of riding time after the autumn equinox is often a blessing in disguise. If you continue to hammer through the winter, you'll be mentally and physically tired when spring rolls around. Winter is an ideal time to recharge your eagerness and develop the types of fitness that cycling doesn't provide. And that's timely advice.

20 SEVEN WAYS TO STAY SLIM THIS WINTER

There is no less physically demanding time for a typical cyclist than winter. Fewer hours of daylight leave less time for riding. And in many areas ice and snow make cycling impossible. The result? Many riders end up wide in the thigh.

To keep from gaining weight this winter, you first have to understand why it happens. The chief reason: age. As you grow older, you gain weight easier. On the average, 60 percent of all calories ingested are used to keep your body breathing and your organs working. But as age slows these basic functions, your body requires fewer calories to maintain them. The result is unused calories and extra weight.

"The majority of energy expended is not in activity, but in your basal metabolic rate—just keeping your body alive," explains Phillip Harvey, Ph.D., a Whittier, California, nutritionist. "Between age 20 and 25, your basal metabolic rate begins to decline by about 2 percent a year. By the time you're in your thirties and forties, your metabolism is much slower than it had been, and it's using significantly fewer calories."

Adds Art Hecker, Ph.D., a Columbus, Ohio, nutritionist: "If you continue to consume your usual amount of calories once your metabolism slows, the excess calories will be deposited as fat. So unless you work harder or reduce your calorie intake you will gain weight."

Ironically, becoming fitter also reduces your caloric needs and increases your chance of weight gain. According to Dr. Harvey, "Training slows your metabolic rate in the same way it reduces your heart rate. When you become fit, you become more efficient at utilizing calories—so you require less."

Each winter, as your age and fitness increase, you're more likely to gain weight. But this doesn't mean you're destined for king-size togs. There are ways to beat the system, and seven ways to stay slim are listed here. Heed each one this winter and you'll feel regenerated, both physically and mentally.

1. Eat less more often. Getting most of your daily calories from a single meal overloads your system and causes rapid weight gain.

"If you consume all your calories in one or two meals

instead of, say, five or more, there's an increase in the amount of fat deposited," explains Dr. Hecker. "It's called the meal-feed syndrome, and many active people do it. They'll eat no breakfast and a light lunch, and then overeat at the end of the day. The body can deal with this intake only to a certain limit, and then excess calories are diverted into fat stores."

2. Monitor your weight. If your weight increases each winter and decreases every spring, the extra poundage gradually gets easier to regain and harder to shed.

"There's a risk to saying, 'Well, okay, I might gain some weight this winter but I'm going to lose it come spring,' " says Dr. Hecker.

"When you have cyclic weight fluctuations, your body retains fat more effectively in anticipation of the expected weight loss. The best way to keep your weight steady is through daily monitoring—when you notice it starting to increase, you can cut back accordingly."

3. Avoid "heavy" foods. These include sauces, dressings, and all fats—fare that's unfortunately most popular during the holidays.

"The type of food people eat in winter is much different than what they eat in summer," says Ann Grandjean, chief nutrition consultant for the U.S. Olympic Committee. "For instance, in winter there's not as much fresh fruit available, and you're not eating as many salads."

A diet that's high in fat literally weighs you down. For instance, eat 100 calories of carbohydrate (a baked potato), and 23 calories are used to process the carbs while the other 77 go into storage. But eat 100 calories of fat (a tablespoon of butter on that baked potato) and only 3 calories are used in combustion while the remaining 97 become fat. For every 3,500 calories unburned, you gain about 1 pound.

4. Drink less alcohol. As the nights grow longer, drinking often replaces other recreational activities. Unfortunately, alcohol is second only to fat as a calorie source.

"One thing it tends to do is make you hungrier," says Dr. Hecker. "You have a few drinks and then you overeat. But more important, alcohol is an 'empty' calorie source. There are no other nutrients coming in with it, unless you're drinking a gin and tonic and eating the lime."

5. Keep riding. Less saddle time is the most obvious reason for winter weight gain. If the roads are too slick for conventional training, try powering a mountain bike through the snow. If you dress correctly, you'll find it fun and invigorating. And you'll burn a lot more calories.

"Not only is the body expending energy for exercise," Dr. Harvey explains, "but it's expending energy just to keep warm."

If the weather is extremely uncooperative, try using an indoor resistance trainer. With such a device, you can re-create an outdoor workout in your living room.

6. Try other sports. According to Grandjean, an ideal alternative for cyclists is swimming. "You'll burn four times as many calories swimming a mile as you will running a mile," she says. "Plus, there's minimal risk of injury."

One caution: Recent research indicates that although swimming promotes fitness, it may actually encourage fat retention—the extra tissue apparently insulates the body against heat loss in cold water.

Cross-country skiing is another winter calorie combustor that taxes many of the same muscles as cycling. Weight training is also worth considering. By spending 3 or 4 hours a week in the gym, you'll not only gain power and strength but also keep your fat levels in check.

7. Don't eat as much. It's as simple as that. If winter means you're exercising less, you should also be eating less. Continue to follow your high-carbo training season diet, but cut back on quantity.

"You can't get away with consuming 4,000 calories a day when your needs drop to 2,500 or 3,000," says Dr. Hecker. "If you want to avoid falling into the winter weight-gain trap, eat less and do more."

Part Four

FITNESS Q&A

21 COMMON FITNESS QUESTIONS

Bicycling is fitness: Ride regularly and you'll lose weight, add muscle, and improve your cardiovascular conditioning. And you get all of these important benefits without the jarring and injury associated with many other sports. But cyclists are not immune to health problems. In fact, there are many fitness questions unique to the sport.

Here are some common endurance-related fitness questions asked by readers of *Bicycling* magazine. The answers are provided by *Bicycling*'s Fitness Advisory Board, a panel of experts in the cycling/health field.

Long Rides Make Him Sick

I'm 38 and have been cycling for three years. I can ride 25 to 35 miles with no problem. But the day after riding 50 to 75 miles, I often experience flulike symptoms, including body aches and dizziness. What causes this?   Doug Merle, Ft. Collins, Colo.

There are three possible explanations: (1) Your muscle soreness is the result of improper conditioning; (2) your muscles are exhausting their fuel stores during the ride (glycogen depletion); or (3) you're not drinking enough, thus lowering blood pressure and encouraging dehydration.

The first solution is straightforward—ride more. To remedy the second, eat a meal rich in carbohydrate (such as pasta), the night before, and nibble throughout the ride. To prevent the third, simply drink more frequently on long rides. All these problems are easily fixed, so there's no reason to limit your mileage.

You might want to experiment with one of the many

Photograph 4-1. The right drink can make the miles go easier.

energy drinks on the market. Drinking a bottle every hour will not only keep your body well hydrated but also supply the carbohydrate your muscles need.   *David L. Smith, M.D.*

Cross-Country Concerns

I'm an adult leader of a Boy Scout troop. Next summer we want to do a bicycle tour of 2,000 to 4,000 miles (possibly the transcontinental Bikecentennial route). We want to average 45 miles a day, or 315 miles a week. We'd like the trip to last 45 to 90 days. The boys range in age from 14 to 18. Can you help us decide upon a training program and the minimum requirements for participation in the tour (i.e., age, previous cycling experience, and so on)? Also, could a trip like this be harmful to the physical development of the boys?   Edward Brandt, Chevy Chase, Md.

Strenuous physical activity at a young age has no known adverse effects on growth and development, as long as there's adequate nourishment. Regarding preparation for such a trip, here are some general thoughts.

Physical differences. With such a wide age group, the physical size and strength of the boys will vary greatly. Some will be prepubertal and others will be ready for the Marines. However, any young person in good health should be able to ride 50 miles or more a day. The stronger boys should carry more supplies on their bikes. I don't think a minimum age is necessary. Many children 13 and younger have ridden cross-country.

Route. Bikecentennial's transcontinental route would be a good choice. It's 4,250 miles, mostly on back roads. Bikecentennial offers maps and organized tours. For information, write: Bikecentennial, Box 8308, Missoula, MT 59807, or call (406) 721-1776.

Bicycles. I've helped oganize similar tours in the past, and usually the boys show up with inappropriate bicycles. Toy-store 10-speeds or BMX-type bikes are not suitable for such a long trip. Most cyclists who ride cross-country do so on bikes costing a minimum of $300. At the very least, your bicycles should have the following equipment.

- Alloy wheels with 27 × 1¼-inch or 700C × 32mm tires.

- Drop handlebars.
- A comfortable leather or high-quality, padded plastic saddle.
- A wide-range gearing system (low of 27 inches or less; high between 90 and 100).
- Good brakes with new pads and well-lubricated cables.
- Sturdy racks (not baskets or homemade devices) for carrying camping equipment.
- Well-adjusted and well-lubricated mechanical components.
- A good fit. This is vital. Perhaps you could talk a local mechanic into having a "bike inspection Saturday" for your group. At the same time, he or she can make sure each bike is in good working condition and fits the rider.

Camping gear. Ordinary backpacking equipment, such as stoves and tents, is suitable for bike tours. The equipment should be carried in bike bags or panniers rather than backpacks.

Training. It should not be difficult for your boys to get in shape for a ride like this. In fact, they'll probably have less difficulty than you. Start with mandatory weekend camping trips of 30 to 40 miles round-trip, then gradually increase the distance. After four or five such trips, the boys should be able to cover 75 miles a day. A few months prior to the cross-country tour, schedule a one-week shakedown trip. This will ensure that everyone is physically and mentally prepared for a few months on the road.

Sag wagon. A Scout trip is best done with an "invisible" sag wagon—the vehicle that carries gear and supplies from campsite to campsite—since the continual sight of one encourages physical and mental laziness. Your vehicle should stay close enough to assist quickly in case of emergency but far enough away to be unseen.

Mileage. Instead of riding 45 miles a day, seven times a week, ride 53 miles a day, six times a week. You'll cover roughly the same distance per week but add more variety to the tour. The rest day could be used for sightseeing, as well as for replenishing spirits and supplies. Good luck.
David L. Smith, M.D.

Seated vs. Upright Climbing

I usually climb in a low gear while seated. I have no trouble keeping up with riders who are out of the saddle in a higher gear. I'm planning a mountainous, one-day ride and have been told that I should learn to ride out of the saddle for long distances. Is this true? What's the best climbing technique?
Stephanie Jay, Seattle, Wash.

In general, the seated position with hands atop the handlebar is more common and efficient and is typically used for long, steady climbing. The standing position, while less efficient, can deliver more power or torque to the pedals and is often used to accelerate through a short change in grade. Riders also stand to change body position and thereby relieve fatigue.

Many cyclists believe that standing is better because your entire body weight is used to pedal. If, however, your weight is being used to push the pedal, then an effort must also be made to pull it back up to the original position. This ultimately requires more energy than seated riding, but it may feel better because the total work, while greater, is shared by muscles of the arms and back.

I recommend experimenting with different climbing positions and practicing making a smooth transition between them. Some riders prefer to shift to a higher gear when they stand. This is appropriate only if you're using a freewheel with closely spaced gears. Whatever you do, don't lock yourself into a climbing position that isn't comfortable just because someone tells you it's better. Find the position that works best for you and use it.   *Steve Johnson, Ph.D.*

Giving Blood

I donate a pint of blood three or four times each year. What effect might this have on my cycling performance? How long does it take to return to predonation performance levels? I have a small build (5 feet 8 inches, 140 pounds), train 150 to 200 miles a week, and am 35 years old.   Robert Mason,
Lake Charles, La.

It takes up to eight weeks for your body to replace a pint of blood. Initially, you can expect a 5 to 10 percent decrease in your exercise capability. You won't notice much of a difference during brief, anaerobic sprints or on long submaximal rides, but your performance in extended "to the max" efforts such as time trials will suffer. Performance should return to normal within two weeks. A more severe risk of donating blood so often is iron deficiency. Have your doctor do a serum ferritin test to determine your iron level. If it's low, start taking an iron supplement or donate blood less frequently.
David L. Smith, M.D.

Flat Hill Training

I'm planning a cycling vacation this summer in Oregon that will include many hilly rides. My normal riding area is almost flat, but there are days when the wind exceeds 10 mph. How does riding into a headwind compare to climbing? Are the techniques used the same? Will my 47-inch low gear be adequate for grades of 5 percent or more? Does drafting help much when climbing?   William Fach, Houston, Tex.

The wind would have to be much stronger than 10 mph to give you the same resistance as climbing a hill. But as long as you're physically fit and properly equipped for a long tour, you shouldn't worry.

To train, include intervals in your program, and perhaps try riding in a 53 × 12 or 54 × 13 gear while out of the saddle on the flats or on a slight uphill. Efforts of this nature will replicate hill riding. In the months preceding your trip, increase the effort from 90 seconds to several minutes and increase the number of repeats every few sessions.

For equipment, a 47-inch gear is adequate unless you'll be climbing long, steep hills or carrying loaded panniers. If so, you might consider adding a triple chainring to your bike or adding a larger cog to the freewheel.

Drafting doesn't help much when climbing, since your speed up the hills isn't high enough to be affected by wind drag. But climbing in a group can be helpful since it gives you a wheel to follow and something to focus on.
Edmund R. Burke, Ph.D.

Becoming a Better Climber

Is there any off-bike training I can do to become a better climber? What about lifting weights and running stairs?
Jeff Singer, Maple Grove, Minn.

Traditional weight lifting (high weight, low repetition) doesn't develop aerobic power or efficiency. Any increase in strength you might realize by following such a program will be offset by the added bulk you'll have to pull uphill. Running stairs, while aerobically beneficial, jars your knees. For the kind of leg strength and lung power you need, stay on the bike and take on the mountains. If you don't have any nearby, you can hone your climbing skills with certain flatland techniques. For instance, some people like to stand up and attack a hill in a relatively high gear, while others (myself included) prefer to shift to a low gear and spin. Good hill training incorporates both these styles. On the flats, alternately practice spinning at 90 to 110 rpm and "honking" out of the saddle in a big gear. Each can be accomplished by simply changing gears. In fact, during the winter, you can practice on an indoor resistance trainer.
Christine L. Wells, Ph.D.

Chairman of the Bored

I'm a 19-year-old male with a problem. When I ride I get bored after approximately 25 miles. In fact, I find myself not wanting to cycle because of it. Please help me.   Mark Beaupre, Tucson, Ariz.

First, vary your route. This will transform tedious rides into new visual experiences. Then turn your casual outings into training rides by adding a series of intervals. Sprint for traffic signs, attack the hills, or pretend you're in a race. This, too, will break the monotony.

Another solution may be to join a local cycling club. Organized tours or training rides with other cyclists are usually more exciting than going alone. Plus, you'll learn about different training techniques and equipment that will contribute to your overall progress. One note of caution, though. In your battle against boredom, avoid wearing stereo headphones. There have been too many accidents involving cyclists who tuned out their environment.   *Edmund R. Burke, Ph.D.*

Upper-Body Power

What weight exercises can I do to increase the strength and endurance of my legs and upper body for cycling?
Jim Bolich, Milton, Pa.

Photograph 4-2. Weight training adds power and strength where cyclists often need it—the upper body. But squats like this build power where it really counts—the legs.

If you want to lift weights, your best bet is to visit a health club or training facility and have a professional devise a custom program. Choose the gym carefully by checking the qualifications of the staff. Be aware that weight training for strength is different than weight training for endurance, so you need to clarify your objectives. Basically, to build strength you should do fewer repetitions with heavier weights. Conversely, to build muscular endurance do more repetitions with lighter weights.

You can also increase upper-body strength at home by using your own body weight as resistance. The best exercises are push-ups, pull-ups, and tricep dips (get between two tables or chairs, place a hand on each, and slowly lower and raise yourself). To build midbody strength, which will help maintain a good riding position, do a few sets of abdominal crunches (lie on your back with your lower legs on a bench or bed, curl your head and shoulders off the floor, reach your hands past your knees, and hold for 3 to 5 seconds) and back extensions (lying on your stomach with your hands on your buttocks, slowly lift your head and shoulders. Hold for 3 to 5 seconds). *Christine L. Wells, Ph.D.*

Endurance Advice

I've been doing light touring for about two years. I started with rides totaling 10 to 15 miles a week, but I'm still doing only 20 to 25 miles a week. Most other amateurs I see or read about ride 50 to 100 miles a week. Whenever I try to do that, my body just says no. Can you give me some advice to help me improve? Todd Ryan, Painesville, Ohio

To improve your ability to tour, you must build your leg strength and endurance, as well as your cardiovascular system. The minimum amount of exercise needed to ensure some cardiovascular improvement is 20 minutes (at an elevated heart rate), four days a week. At beginning touring pace, this equals about 16 miles weekly. It's considered safe to increase this mileage about 20 percent each week. When you can comfortably ride for 45 minutes, four days a week, begin sprinkling in quality workouts such as intervals and hill repeats.

Remember that to improve athletically, you must be persistent and systematic. If your body keeps saying no, you might consider seeing a physician or exercise physiologist in order to determine your aerobic capabilities.   *Andrew L. Pruitt, M.S.*

24-Hour Ride

For more than a year I've been possessed by the idea of cycling 300 miles in 24 hours. I have completed several centuries and a double century and have no doubt that with a little luck and lots of hard training, I can pass this new milestone, too.

I would appreciate any tips regarding proper nutrition and water intake for a ride lasting this long. Any tips on riding at night would also be helpful. In fact, any advice that might prevent me from collapsing before reaching mile 299 would be welcome.   Tom Chamberlin, Arlington, Va.

If I were trying to ride 300 miles in 24 hours, I'd plan on resting about 10 minutes every 2 hours. This means I'd be riding 22 of 24 hours and would have to average 13.6 mph to reach my goal. Because it's dangerous to ride at night when fatigued, I'd start at sundown. Besides arranging for a support vehicle and mounting lights on my bicycle, I'd also wear an ANSI-approved helmet.

To prevent dehydration, proper fluid replacement is essential during a marathon ride. Drink one or two bottles of water every hour, depending on the temperature. Drink even though you may not be thirsty. A bottle or two of an energy drink might also be beneficial for maintaining your body fuels. There are many such drinks on the market. Pick the one that tastes best.

In preparation, I'd carbo-load for about three days prior to the ride by eating lots of pasta and fresh vegetables. During the ride, munch on something solid about every 2 hours. The old standards are bananas, apples, oranges, granola bars, oatmeal cookies, bread, cheese, and sandwiches. You'll need lots of calories, so don't skimp. But be careful not to overeat, since it can leave you feeling sluggish. To guard against any intestinal

surprises, use training rides to become accustomed to the fluids and foods you plan to use in the marathon.
Christine L. Wells, Ph.D.

Heat and Humidity

In baseball, they talk of the ball not traveling as well in hot, humid conditions. I suppose the thinking is that the heavier the air, the more difficult it is for the ball to move through it. While struggling home in 90 degree, 90 percent humidity the other day, I got to wondering if I was experiencing the same thing. Does the air offer more resistance to a cyclist when it's filled with moisture or is it merely an illusion compounded by the heat?   Jose Kitz, Schnecksville, Pa.

Your question is a complex one, since heat and humidity not only affect air density (as you suggest) but also the body's physiology.

As the air warms, it expands and becomes less dense. Surprisingly, rising humidity has a similar effect. This is because water molecules push aside the heavier oxygen and nitrogen molecules. Contrary to popular belief, baseballs and bicycles actually move *more* quickly through hot, humid air. The difference, however, is small and variable. A more important factor is the decline in air density with altitude. This is why many cycling records are set in such places as Colorado Springs and Mexico City. Although a cyclist has less available oxygen at such heights, the disadvantage this poses is outweighed by the reduction in air resistance.

Still, why do we struggle when it's hot and humid? During strenuous exercise our body generates tremendous amounts of heat. In fact, during cycling only about 25 percent of our energy is used for propulsion. The rest goes into the furnace. To avoid severe consequences, namely heatstroke and even death, our body must quell this physiological fire. Normally, this is done through the evaporation of perspiration.

However, when humidity is high, evaporation is hindered. Nevertheless, the body responds by sending more blood to the skin to encourage even more perspiration. The effects are twofold: There's less blood for the working muscles, and our body becomes dehydrated and overheated. Both reduce performance. To minimize such debilitating effects and make cycling in hot, humid conditions less of a struggle, carry extra water, drink frequently, and pace yourself.   *David P. Swain, Ph.D.*

Getting Started

I'm 23 years old and have never been very physically active. My husband is putting together a custom bicycle for me, but before I begin cycling I'd like some advice. I'm 5 feet 6 inches, 115 pounds, and have never had any major medical problems. What's the best way to work into a cycling program? My goal is to enjoy the sport while getting myself into good physical shape. Mary Rachel Bogan, Dallas, Tex.

Start by riding 10 miles, four times a week at a cadence of 75 revolutions per minutes (rpm). There are a number of cycle-computers on the market that record elapsed time, distance, velocity, cadence, and the like. They're fun to use and helpful for someone who likes to go at things systematically. Gradually increase the length of your rides to 20 miles and your cadence to 85 to 90 rpm. Eventually, incorporate a couple of 50-mile rides into your monthly training program.

You might find it best not to ride with your husband at first. He'll probably want to ride faster than you, which might prove discouraging. Go at your own pace. I'm assuming that your custom bicycle fits you properly. Just remember not to push too high a gear, but rather to spin in a low gear and build endurance gradually.   *Christine L. Wells, Ph.D.*

Staying Hydrated

How much should I drink during a ride? Is it possible to drink too much?   John Rutledge, El Cajon, Calif.

The amount and type of solution a rider should drink depends on two factors: (1) the need to offset dehydration; and (2) the need to supplement the body's limited carbohydrate stores. Two water bottles per hour (one bottle equals 20 ounces or about 600 ml) is about as much as most people can tolerate, but everyone must experiment to find his or her limit. A general recommendation is to drink 6 to 12 ounces every 15 to 30 minutes. Although there have been rare reports of endurance athletes overdiluting important body fluids by drinking large amounts of water, generally the only risk you run in drinking too much is feeling bloated or sick.

For rides less than 2 hours, water is all you need. On warm days when you sweat more, drink as much as possible. The less dehydrated your body becomes, the less fatigued you'll feel. Remember also that a cool drink is not only more refreshing, it empties from the stomach into the bloodstream faster.

For rides longer than 2 hours, it's best to drink solutions containing sugar or starch. These delay fatigue by keeping the body's carbohydrate stores high. Commercial energy or sports drinks, for instance, contain 6 to 10 percent carbohydrate. This is present in the form of glucose, glucose polymers (starches), or table sugar (sucrose). Fruit juices, which primarily contain fruit sugar or fructose, are not as effective because they don't convert as quickly into energy.

TABLE 4-1.
Energy Drinks

Name	Carbohydrate (%)	Type of Carbohydrate
Recharge	7.6	Fructose, glucose
Max	7.5	Glucose polymers, fructose
Exceed	7.0	Glucose polymers, fructose
Isostar	7.0	Sucrose, glucose, fructose
Gatorade	6.0	Sucrose, glucose
Gookinaid E.R.G.	5.0	Glucose
BodyFuel	4.5	Glucose polymers

Since it takes time for carbohydrate solutions to work, you should begin drinking 30 to 60 minutes into a long ride. These mixtures also empty more slowly from the stomach, so the total amount ingested should be reduced to 5 to 10 ounces every 15 to 30 minutes. Table 4-1 shows some popular energy drinks and their carbohydrate concentration. Do some experimenting to find one that suits your tastes and needs.
Edward F. Coyle, Ph.D.

Preride Insomnia

Why can't I get a good night's sleep before my annual double century ride? After a sleepless night I'm so tired at the start that I say to myself, "Only 200 miles then you can get some sleep." I'll soon be riding my 17th double century, and this time I'd like to be well rested.   Stephen E. Halton, Carmichael, Calif.

Athletes often have difficulty getting a good night's sleep before a major competition. The reasons range from anxiety to excitement.

I suggest you integrate a relaxation exercise into your preride schedule. A typical exercise usually takes about 20 minutes. Start by lying on your bed and taking long, deep breaths. Count slowly from one to five and close your eyes. Next, tighten and loosen each muscle group from your head to your toes. Begin with your forehead and proceed to your jaws, neck, shoulders, arms, stomach, buttocks, thighs, calves, and feet. Flex and relax each muscle group twice.

By this time, you should feel physically relaxed. Next, visualize yourself in a peaceful environment such as the beach or the mountains. Let yourself absorb the positive scenery. This should allow you to drift off to sleep. If you have trouble doing this on your own, audio relaxation tapes might help.
Andrew Jacobs, Ph.D.

Sleeping Toes

My toes fall asleep about 2 hours into a ride. I've changed shoes, but the problem persists. What should I do?   Tony De Almeida, Pasadena, Calif.

Loosen your shoes. It's that simple, although it took me years of riding with toes that tingled, burned, throbbed, and eventually went numb to figure it out. I even squirted water into my shoes to put out the "fire."

The problem is actually caused when feet swell during a ride, eventually making shoes too tight. This puts pressure on nerves and reduces blood circulation, which together result in numbness. My feet today are as accurate as an odometer: By 70 miles, they're uncomfortable enough to make me stop and loosen the laces.   *John Kukoda*

Knee Problems

Whenever I ride fast (18 mph or more) for extended periods, I experience pain in my knees. This does not happen if I ride slowly in a low gear. Last year I rode 4,500 miles, including many 100- and 200-mile days. After this much training, shouldn't my knees be able to handle the strain?   Dave Frantz, St. Louis Park, Minn.

Your knee pain could stem from any number of things, ranging from the abrasion of tendons to roughness behind the kneecaps. But before subjecting yourself to a costly medical exam, try these possible solutions.

First, make sure your bicycle is properly adjusted. Have a professional mechanic ensure that it fits you.

Second, when riding, use low gears whenever possible. Turning a big gear can stress problem knees. And third, rework your training schedule. All those 100- and 200-mile days might be taking their toll. Ride shorter distances, more often.

And while it's true that racers subject their knees to a great deal of stress, many never encounter knee problems. It depends on the individual.   *James C. Holmes, M.D.*

Gearing Up

I'm 22, and have been averaging more than 1,200 miles each of the past few summers. I've got a 12-speed bike, and I'm always on the big gears (52 × 16). I've been told that such gears could

*be harmful to my knees, and that I should use a larger freewheel
cog with my large chainring in order to increase my spinning.
But I'm already doing 90 rpm, and even more, in a 52 × 16.
What should I do?*   Sylvain Berube, Laval, Quebec

Pushing gears too big for your strength can be harmful to your
knees, especially the quadriceps tendon, patella (kneecap),
and patella tendon. But if you can spin 90 rpm in a 52 × 16 or
larger, that's a statement of your strength and you should be
okay. If your cadence falls below 90 rpm, though, don't be
embarrassed to shift to a lower gear.
    Every serious cyclist should learn to spin 90 rpm or greater,
as you're doing. It's efficient and healthy. However, remember
there are situations when you want to turn your legs slower,
such as climbing out of the saddle or sitting in a big pack
resting your legs for the next hard effort.
    As with any strenuous exercise, you should approach big
gears gradually regardless of strength. Increase your time,
intensity, and distance as your body allows. And to spot knee
trouble, watch for discomfort around the kneecap that doesn't
go away when you cut back the intensity of your effort.
Andrew L. Pruitt, M.S.

Constant Cadence

*Most cycling literature I've read recommends maintaining steady
cadence and heart rate during endurance rides, but I find this
difficult to do—especially when riding into a head wind or
climbing. Should I continue to try to keep my cadence constant
thoughout a day's tour, or should I let it vary with conditions?*
Weldon Young, Windsor Junction, Nova Scotia

If your goal is endurance or extended touring, it's best to keep
cadence and pulse relatively constant. When you're confronted
by hills or head winds, just shift to a lower gear to keep your
cadence at optimal levels. Allow the extra work to slow you
down, keeping your heart rate constant. This doesn't mean
you should always strive to keep cadence or pulse constant.
You should occasionally sprint up hills or go on short, fast rides
to give yourself nonendurance (speed) workouts. You may
find the variety adds enjoyment to your cycling.
David P. Swain, Ph.D.

Back in the Saddle

I'm 41 years old, 5 feet 9 inches, and weigh 200 pounds. I ride my Raleigh Olympian 12-speed on an erratic basis. Some weeks I won't ride at all, others, I'll total 100 miles. But I've never gone more than 50 miles on a single outing. Last year, in order to relieve strain on a previously sprained back, I reangled my bicycle seat. While attempting my first century, I couldn't even complete my usual 50 miles. At 20 miles I began having pain in the crotch area, and at 36 miles I had to drop out. I missed a week of work and had to take anti-inflammatory drugs.

As I return to cycling, how can I figure the correct seat angle to avoid more back or bottom pain? Would it help if I had a consistent training schedule?   Gregory T. Rollberg, Frankfort, Ill.

Reposition your saddle so it's level with the top tube, or tipped up slightly in front. And to lessen the strain on your back, raise the handlebar stem. Keep it no more than four to five centimeters below the top of the saddle. In your case it may be more comfortable if it's level with the top of the saddle. Just don't exceed the maximum-height line on the stem. In addition, make sure the stem length and seat height are correct for your body. I suggest having someone at your local bike shop fit the bike to you.

Bicycle saddles are like running shoes—you have to find the one that's most comfortable for you. You may want to slip a padded cover over the saddle you already have, or experiment with any of the new gel-filled saddles. Many riders find them more comfortable.

Finally, consistent riding will make centuries easier and injuries less likely. Just don't push it. Allow your body to slowly become accustomed to the sport.
Edmund R. Burke, Ph.D.

What Is a Balanced Diet?

I'm 18 years old and weigh 200 pounds. I started cycling to lose weight and get in shape for football. I love it, but I don't think I'm getting all the nutrients I need from my diet of oranges, cheese, and crackers.   Marc Montnaye, Omaha, Nebr.

Losing weight and eating properly is not difficult if you follow some basic rules. A diet of oranges, cheese, and crackers is not only nutritionally unbalanced, but may also be too high in fat. Your diet should consist of a variety of foods from the four basic food groups. It should also be high in complex carbohydrates (starch and fiber) and low in fat. Because you're active you'll automatically lose weight on this type of diet.

I recommend approximately 2,000 calories a day. You should include the following: two servings from the milk group (1 cup milk, 1½ slices cheese, 1 cup yogurt, 1 cup cottage cheese, 1¾ cups ice cream); two servings from the meat group (2 ounces lean red meat, fish, or poultry, 2 eggs, 1 cup beans, 4 tablespoons peanut butter); eight servings from the vegetable group (½ cup cooked vegetables, 1 cup raw vegetables, ½ cup fruit juice, 1 piece fresh fruit); eight servings from the grain group (1 cup cereal, 1 slice bread, ½ cup pasta, 1 pancake, 1 muffin). You should also take a multivitamin and mineral supplement.   *Phillip W. Harvey, Ph.D., R.D.*

CREDITS

The information in this book is drawn from these and other articles in *Bicycling* Magazine.

"Be Your Own Coach" Fred Matheny, "Be Your Own Coach," April 1987.

"Getting Ready to Ride" Fred Matheny, "Spring Tune-Up," May 1987.

"Olympic Stretching for Your Body and Mind" Mark Gorski, "Stretch Your Body and Your Mind," February 1988.

"Training for a Century" Fred Zahradnik, "Training for a Century," August 1987.

"Training for a Double Century" Chris Kostman, "Training for a Double Century," April 1989.

"Training for a Tour" John Kukoda, "Get Ready to Ride," April 1987.

"Fifteen Ways to Maximize Endurance" Fred Zahradnik, "Training for a Century," August 1987.

"Making Every Ride Great" Nelson Pena, "How to Make Every Ride a Great One," July 1989.

"All about Saddle Sores" Steve Johnson, Ph.D., "Saddle Sores," October/November 1989.

"Perfect Positions" Connie Carpenter Phinney, "Long-Distance Comfort," August 1988; Geoff Drake and John Kukoda, "Perfect Positions," March 1990.

"Reaching Your Potential" Michael Shermer, "Master of My Fate," June 1989.

"Food for Fuel" Nelson Pena, "What Does This Man Know That You Don't?" July 1988.

"Meals on Wheels" Nelson Pena, "Meals on Wheels," May 1987.

"Different Rides, Different Diets" Liz Applegate, Ph.D., "Different Rides, Different Diets," July 1988.

"Twinkie Power" Ellen Coleman, M.S., R.D., "Twinkie Power," August 1989.

"All about Body Fat" Fred Matheny, "Body Fat," August 1987.

"Minimum Workouts for Maximum Fitness" Fred Matheny, "The Least You Can Do," May 1988.

"Total Fitness" Fred Matheny, "Totally Fit," April 1988.

"A Winter Training Program" Fred Matheny, "Stay Fit for Cycling in Six Hours a Week," December 1987.

"Seven Ways to Stay Slim This Winter" Joe Kita and Nelson Pena, "Eat, Drink, but Be Wary," December 1987.

"Common Fitness Questions" "Fitness Q&A," various issues.

Photographs

Donna M. Chiarelli: photos 1-1, 1-2, 1-3, 1-4, and 3-2; Mitch Mandel: photo 1-5; John P. Hamel: photo 1-6; Angelo M. Caggiano: photo 2-1; Sally Shenk Ullman: photo 3-1; Robert Gerheart: photo 4-1; Christie C. Tito: photo 4-2.

Rodale Press, Inc., publishes BICYCLING, America's leading cycling magazine. For information on how to order your subscription, write to BICYCLING, Emmaus, PA 18098.